'Arguments about God, including the New Atheism debate, usually generate more heat than light. *The God Debate* is a notable and welcome exception: it offers an objective but engaged overview of the basic issues, and points toward an alternative to both religious fundamentalism and scientific fundamentalism.'

Dr. David Loy, author of *Money, Sex, War, Karma: Notes for a Buddhist Revolution*

'Does God exist? This book gives the answer by cleverly avoiding to answer the question. But it gives us a concise review of the varied history of the pro and contra. It also inspires the question (without answering it) whether it might be worthwhile to consider the possibility of the existence of something we used to call god – a something that we vainly try to grasp with our imagination, or to refute with our reason.'

Stephan Schumacher, author of *Zen in Plain English*

'Gerald Benedict's *The God Debate* gives serious weight and attention both to the new atheists and to those who have shown that religion is far more sophisticated than the version those atheists denounce. Benedict presents us with a sweeping and useful philosophical introduction to the current state of the debate in ways that lead us to see why neither side will ever "win" because each starts from such different conceptions of what is meant by "God" and by "reason".'

Rabbi Michael Lerner, editor, *Tikkun* magazine, author *Embracing Israel/Palestine*

'Gerald Benedict has sought to bring to the present "God debate" a reasoned, and imaginative series of arguments and reflections born out of a lifetime of teaching. *The God Debate* brings a welcome perspective on matters of belief and truth.'

The Rt. Rev. Peter Price, Bishop of Bath and Wells

'An erudite and timely overview of the polarized debates between religious theorists and the promoters of atheism. The author provides a thoughtful and concise summary of the principal arguments and issues and asks whether science and religion are mutually exclusive or whether recent scientific developments point the way to more meaningful dialogue.'

Michael Barnes: former senior producer, BBC Science and Features Department

The GOD DEBATE

A New Look at History's Oldest Argument

GERALD BENEDICT

WATKINS PUBLISHING
LONDON

This edition published in the UK and USA in 2013 by
Watkins Publishing Limited, Sixth Floor,
75 Wells Street, London W1T 3QH

A member of Osprey Group

Text Copyright © Gerald Benedict 2013
Design and typography Copyright © Watkins Publishing Limited 2013

Gerald Benedict has asserted his right under the
Copyright, Designs and Patents Act 1988 to be
identified as the author of this work.

1 3 5 7 9 10 8 6 4 2

Designed and typeset by Donald Sommerville

Printed and bound in Italy by L.E.G.O.

A CIP record for this book is available from the British Library

ISBN: 978-1-78028-563-4

www.watkinspublishing.co.uk

Distributed in the USA and Canada by Sterling Publishing Co., Inc.
387 Park Avenue South, New York, NY 10016-8810

For information about custom editions, special sales,
premium and corporate purchases, please contact
Sterling Special Sales Department at 800-805-5489
or specialsales@sterlingpub.com

For Roger and Merril Nunn

'Don't walk in front of me, I may not follow.
Don't walk behind me, I may not lead.
Just walk beside me and be my friend.'
            Albert Camus

Contents

Acknowledgements

THERE ARE SEVERAL PEOPLE who have generously contributed in different ways to the writing of this book. As
always I'm greatly indebted to my friend, publisher and
commissioning editor, Michael Mann, for his guidance and
encouragement. I owe my copy-editor, Donald Sommerville, and indexer, Charmian Parkin, huge thanks for
ensuring the book is, in every respect, in good condition.
Michael D Jacobson, who died during the editing process,
is gratefully remembered as a friend and constant adviser
on all aspects of the writing. Richard Nethercotte, the Rev.
Roger Nunn and Judge Andrew Woolman have read and
advised on substantial sections of the text. My daughters,
Noémie and Amélie, challengingly considered parts of
the text from the student point of view, and I'm further
indebted to Amélie for her copious research for sources,
and for tracking down the books of publishers now extinct.

I am grateful to the editor of the on-line *Stamford
Encyclopedia of Philosophy* for being willing to let me
quote from this very valuable source; to Maureen Gamble
for the quote from her Wichita State University thesis
'Psychology and Experience'; to *First Things* for the quote
from Professor Paul Davies's Templeton Prize acceptance
address in their August/September 1995 edition; to the
Yale and Chicago Presses for the extract taken from *God's
Undertaker* by John Lennox, published by Lion Hudson
plc. 2007, copyright 2007, John Lennox. My thanks also

go to Darren Scott at HardPress for permission to quote from Schopenhauer's *On Religion, a Dialogue etc.*; to Sarah MacMahon for the quote from *The Future of an Illusion*, taken from Volume 21 of *The Standard Edition of the Complete Psychological Works of Sigmund Freud*, translated and edited by James Strachey, published by the Hogarth Press; to the Jewish Publication Society of America for the quotation from Rabbi Joseph B Soloveitchik's *Halakhic Man*. Sarah Dobson at Polity Books kindly gave permission for me to use quotations from Alain Badiou's *Philosophy in the Present*, and C S Lewis Pte. Ltd. generously gave permission for the quotation from *Surprised by Joy*, by C S Lewis, copyright 1955. Biblical quotations have been taken from: *Tanakh*, Jewish Publication Society, 1985; *The Holy Scriptures*, Koren Publishers, Jerusalem, English text revised and edited by Harold Fisch, 1988; *Holy Bible*, Revised Standard Version, Eyre and Spottis-woode, London, 1952 & 1971; *The New English Bible*, Oxford and Cambridge University Presses, 1970.

These acknowledgments would not be complete without expressing my deep gratitude to my wife, Nadège. Her constant support, patience and encouragement ensured the book was completed.

I have made every effort to secure permissions for copy-righted material and will be pleased to make good any omissions brought to my attention in future printings of this book.

'We must follow the argument wherever it leads.'
Socrates

'Go on, believe! It does no harm.'
Ludwig Wittgenstein

———◦∘◦———

Introduction

> 'Human reason has this fate that in one species of knowledge it is burdened by questions which, as prescribed by the very nature of reason itself, it is not able to ignore, but which, as transcending all its power, it is also not able to answer.'
>
> *Zaid Shakir*

IN HIS REVIEW for the *Guardian* (8 December 2007) of John Lennox's *God's Undertaker: Has Science Buried God?* Colin Tudge wrote, 'There is no more important debate than this – science versus religion.' While the existence of God has always been debated, the present and considerable rise in interest has been stimulated by the 'New Atheism'. This takes the view that religion in all its forms should no longer be tolerated, but discarded as irrelevant because it is incompatible with science and rational thought. Accordingly, religion must be opposed wherever it has influence. The New Atheists have been vigorously led by a group which has included the evolutionary biologist Richard Dawkins, the author and journalist Christopher Hitchens, the philosopher and cognitive scientist Daniel C Dennet, the neuroscientist Sam Harris, and the particle physicist V J Stenger. Theists engaging the New Atheists in the debate include John Carson Lennox, a Fellow in Mathematics and Philosophy of Science at Green Templeton College, Oxford University, John Polkinghorne, a theoretical physicist and theologian and Professor of Mathematical Physics at the University of Cambridge, Paul Davies, a physicist, writer and broadcaster and professor at Arizona State University, and philosophers such as Anthony Flew, Mark C Taylor and the literary theorist and critic Terry Eagleton, Professor of English Literature at the University of Lancaster.

The main thrust of the debate appears to be the perennial argument between science and religion, but the issues are by no means neatly confined to these two disciplines. While there are eminent scientists who deny the existence of God, there are others who are equally convinced that God does exist, but the same divide is found among scholars of other disciplines such as philosophy, psychology, anthropology and history.

An alternative and increasingly respectable position is that of the agnostic. Although the English biologist T H Huxley, who was known as 'Darwin's Bulldog', coined the word 'agnosticism' in 1869, the concept has a very long history. From the Greek, the term literally means, 'without gnosis', that is, 'without knowledge'. While atheists regard a belief in the existence of God as rationally untenable, agnostics hold the view that it is impossible ever to know whether or not God does exist. Traditionally, agnosticism holds the middle ground between theism and atheism.

The debate is involved and multifaceted, drawing on many different disciplines. It addresses numerous concepts of God taken from both Western and Eastern religion, it draws on the philosophies of science, religion and history, on theories of knowledge, on psychology and anthropology, but its basic concern is simply stated – is there a God or isn't there? The arguments set out to demonstrate, one way or another, the absolute truth of an absolute being, or to consign such an idea to the realm of fantasy, myth and superstition. Concepts of gods, or a God, have been with us since the earliest human communities; developed as religion they have had a determining influence on the formation of civilizations and cultures, and on how people have tried to understand the origin, meaning and purpose of life. Originally, as we shall see, the debate was the concern of philosophers and theologians, but the ground has changed to a debate about the nature of knowledge, about how we can be sure that what we claim to know is true or false, and how to demonstrate or prove this. In this process science has taken a leading part, setting out objective principles that can test the truth of anything claimed as 'knowledge'.

The debate is not only about the existence of one, supreme God, or of many gods, but also about whether anything metaphysical, that is something without material form or substance, can be said to exist. If we want to claim such an existence in any meaningful way, that claim would need to be rationally verified. It is held that 'real' knowledge, the kind we can be sure about, is gained only through our sense experience, that is to say empirically, a position philosophy terms 'Empiricism'. Experience, however, includes those of a religious or spiritual nature. Abraham Maslow, a professor of psychology at Brandies University, suggested that 'spiritual life is part of the human essence. It is a defining characteristic of human nature without which human nature is not fully human nature.' If this is true, then the ground of religion is to be found *within* human nature and Alexander Pope's counsel, 'Know then thyself, presume not God to scan; The proper study of mankind is Man,' would lead us to a knowledge of God, as well as of ourselves. It is a perception shared by certain Eastern religious traditions.

Anyone can claim that their spiritual life amounts to authentic experience and as such argue that it is built-in to human nature. The problem is how to objectivize this. Can the subjectivism of a personal experience be communicated in a way that would convince others of its truth? We might be able to accept that someone's experience is genuine, but is so only for them; for ourselves to recognize it as genuine, we would need to have a similar experience. Atheists are atheists because they find the claims made for subjective experience of this kind are untenable as a basis for truth. Believers are believers because the experience itself is, for them, sufficient evidence of its authenticity. Austin Farrer, an English theologian and philosopher, wrote, 'The issue between the atheist and the believer is not whether it makes sense to question ultimate fact, it is rather the question, what fact is ultimate? The atheist's ultimate fact is the universe; the theist's ultimate fact is God.'

The current form of the debate begins with this impasse, the conflict between scientific and theological orthodoxy. It is argued that theological orthodoxy narrows the terms of reference in which the debate takes place. To argue, on the one hand, that the Bible is literally true, places the narrowest construction on the points at issue; to claim, on the other hand, that its central stories, for example, the Genesis account of creation, Noah's flood, the virgin birth and the resurrection of Jesus are myths that contain truth 'of another kind', offers ground for a more open-ended discussion. But it is argued that scientific orthodoxy, particularly its precise principles of proof, also narrows the terms of reference in which the discussion takes place. Atheists consider that theists fall back on the God-hypothesis to fill gaps in their knowledge; but there are considerable gaps in scientific knowledge and important questions to which science, as yet, can make no response. It can tell us about the universe, its origins, character and the laws that sustain it, but it cannot tell us why the universe or ourselves are here; nor can it tell us about meaning and purpose, about values and tastes, about suffering and what is termed 'evil', and about whether or not we have some form of free will. Atheism makes a strong case for religion being founded on unverifiable claims, but science also trades on articles of faith as does any source of knowledge. In *Sources of the Self,* the philosopher Charles Taylor wrote, 'to hold that there are no assumptions in a scientist's work which aren't already based on evidence is surely a reflection of a blind faith, one that can't even feel the occasional tremor of doubt'.

There are several reasons why the debate is of increasing importance. Firstly, the arguments make us face questions of ultimate significance. For this reason, there is urgent need to see if there are alternatives to the irreconcilable views of atheists and theists. As mentioned above, there is nothing new about this debate; humankind has always been faced with issues of ultimate importance, but it is made urgent in our own times by what biological scientists and astrophysicists are saying about the origins both of the universe and the life of our planet. Until now there has been an uneasy co-existence between science and religion, the former tolerating the presence and influence of religion while pointing to its irrational shortcomings. Religion has either been in denial of the knowledge disclosed by science or, in various ways, as will be shown in the following chapters, has tried to accommodate and adapt to it. Today, the fundamental differences have become more sharply defined. More emphatically than ever before atheists regard religion as a subversive influence, something which in Hitchens's term, 'poisons everything'. In response, fundamentalist religion has taken refuge by creeping deeper into its doctrines, holding uncompromisingly, for example, to a creationist view of the origins of everything, while more liberal religious attitudes are reconsidering their understanding of God in the light of what science has disclosed about 'God's creation'.

Secondly, the debate is made urgent because of the opposing atheist–theist views about the increasing secularization of society. Atheists would like to reduce, or even eliminate, the influence of religion, especially with regard to the establishment of the Church, politics, education, law and, more generally, morality. The extent of the influence of religion varies from country to country; England retains its established Church of England, with its twenty-six senior bishops, the Lords Spiritual, sitting in the British House of Lords, and religious education remains a core-curriculum subject in state schools throughout the UK. The atheist lobby pushes for a wholly secular society, as exists, for example in France, where there is no established religion and where religious education is banned from state schools in favour of '*éducation civique, juridique et sociale*'. Religious education for children is available within the religious communities, or in private religious schools. Some states in the USA are, in this respect, similar to France.

Thirdly, the debate is important because of the 'lamentable state' in which society now finds itself, 'I mean by "lamentable state",' writes Terry Eagleton, 'the prevalence of greed, idolatry, and delusion, the depth of our instinct to dominate and possess, the dull persistence of injustice and exploitation, the chronic anxiety which leads us to hate, maim, and exploit, along with sickness, suffering, and despair . . .' The New Atheists argue that a secular humanism can better address these issues than can religion; theists argue that only the ethical and moral standards of religion can offer solutions to these problems. Because the lines between the opposed views have become hard-edged and sharply drawn, the debate faces us with a stark choice – which has the better case, scientific rationalism or religion? The debate also requires us to consider if these conflicting alternatives are carved in stone, or if, as the closing chapter of the book suggests, there is a possibility of a broader, more open-minded middle ground which allows both parties to engage in creative rather than polemical thinking.

There are many books that present the arguments of both atheists and theists, whatever their specialist discipline might be. A selected list of these books is given in 'Further Reading'. There are very few books that, remaining neutral, survey the arguments of both sides; the purpose of this book is not to bring the reader to any specific conclusion, but to outline and discuss the principal arguments and points of view of those who have brought the debate into the media glare.

Having in the opening chapters described what is at the heart of the debate – the concept of God, its origins and meaning – the book continues by discussing the main issues; all the important subjects of the debate are treated, and the underlying concepts such as faith and knowledge, knowledge and belief, and the nature of religious experience are fully explained. Atheism is shown in various conjunctions: atheism *v.* religion; atheism *v.* the concept of faith, whether or not that faith is attached to a specific religious tradition; atheism *v.* God, whether or not that God is the monotheistic God of the Bible, or an indefinable concept drawn from animism, polytheism or a more general pantheism. Atheism is also considered over against the more abstract, non-credal notions of God that lie within mysticism, the Mind–Body–Spirit movements and New Age religions.

Any debate is always more interesting and satisfying when the protagonists are carefully considering, with at least some degree of open-mindedness, what the other has to say. However, the 'God-debate' mostly takes the form of strongly presented arguments when nothing is conceded and no ground is given, in which one argument is set against another in much the same way as on the political hustings. There is great and urgent need for a better quality of discussion. There was little conceded in the famous debate on the existence of God broadcast by the BBC in 1948, between the philosopher Bertrand Russell and the Jesuit priest Father Frederick C Copleston. This debate was not between a theist and a scientist, but a philosopher and a philosophical theologian, and it remains a model in as much as due and careful consideration was given by each to the arguments of the other.

It is possible that if the debate continues creatively, what may eventually emerge will be a synthesis of the opposed views, a syncretism of theistic philosophy and scientific theory. Such a synthesis has already been attempted by, for example, the Jesuit philosopher and palaeontologist Teilhard de Chardin, who introduced us to the significance of the 'noosphere', the collective interaction of human minds; more recently, Ken Wilbur proposed what he called an 'Integral Theory', 'to draw together an already existing number of separate paradigms into an interrelated network of approaches that are mutually enriching'. Another interesting and important synthesis is given by the physicist Fritjof Capra in his book *The Tao of Physics: An Exploration of the Parallels Between Modern Physics and Eastern Mysticism*. The final chapter of this book, Chapter 8, 'God and a Theory of Everything', discusses the ideas concerned with these kinds of syntheses.

It may be an urban legend, but there is an account of an 18th-century debate convened in St Petersburg by Catherine the Great. She called together the renowned Swiss mathematician Leonhard Euler and the French atheist philosopher Denis Diderot. Both Diderot and the court of Catherine the Great, were astounded when Euler approached the philosopher and said, 'Sir, $(a+bn)/n=x$, hence God exists. Reply!' Diderot was embarrassed; he had no reply and the court dissolved in laughter. If proving God's existence was that simple, the current debate, like that of Catherine's court, would be concluded. The atheist lobby does not ask believers to produce a mathematical formula that proves the existence of God, but it does require some form of objective demonstration without which they hold the God-hypothesis to be untenable. The present debate pivots on whether or not there are valid grounds for believing in God's existence even though no such objective proof can be given.

That the debate takes place at all is testimony to the enduring belief in God's existence. Despite the demise of traditional religion, it seems that large numbers of people of all cultures either hold to a belief in some form of God, or are engaged in the quest for that belief. It is hoped that this book will contribute to the debate; it is not a polemic, but an overview of the essential issues given in such a way that will allow the reader to assess the strength of the arguments. That done, a stand can be made for or against the God-hypothesis, or on the agnostic middle ground.

Author's Note

In debating the existence of God, the atheists' case focuses somewhat specifically on Christianity, and in discussing the arguments of both sides it will be apparent that this book carries a similar emphasis. However, in having such a precise agenda the atheists may well have overlooked some significant issues since Eastern religions, for example, offer radically different concepts of the Absolute and metaphysics than those held in the West. There are also marked differences between Christianity and the other biblical religions. For this reason, where necessary, essential concepts of the debate are drawn from other religious traditions, for example, those of

Judaism, Islam, Hinduism and Buddhism. It is hoped that these contributions will widen and enrich the discourse. However, to have written about the debate on the God-hypothesis in a way that would do full justice to the philosophies and perceptions of these other faiths, would have required a far longer book.

Chapter One

The God-Hypothesis –
Its Evolution and Variety

THE 'GOD-HYPOTHESIS' IS SOMETHING of a pantechnicon term carrying an almost unlimited variety of ideas. In the West, 'God' is broadly understood, by both believers and atheists, to refer to some form of ultimate, all-powerful being, the creator of everything that exists, who has the familiar attributes of omniscience, omnipotence and omni-presence. For some God exists as a remote and unintrusive presence, while others experience a direct, personal relationship that involves every aspect of their lives. Atheists argue that such a being does not exist; God is a concept grounded in mythology, a subject of fantasy and delusion, at best an extended metaphor used to fill the gaps in our knowledge.

Traditionally, atheism is a philosophical rational rejec-tion of belief in the existence of any form of deity, or supernaturalism. Today, the conventional arguments for atheism have been given new impetus by the black-hole, multiple-universe cosmology of the new astrophysics, and the DNA-based evolutionary account of the origin and development of life disclosed by the biological sciences. For scientists, the quest is not for a God but for a 'theory of everything', which Stephen Hawking said, if discovered, would 'be the ultimate triumph of human reason – for then we should know the mind of God'. Both the scientific and philosophical quest for a theory of everything is a hugely ambitious undertaking, but one in which, in different ways, human beings have always engaged.

An account of the origins of the God-hypothesis and the many forms it takes is a subject that has occupied entire books and only an overview can be given here of what are predominantly Western religious concepts, although reference will be made to Eastern traditions and to the very different concepts of God they represent.

The discussion is set out under two headings: From Polytheism to Monotheism, and The God of the Philosophers.

1. From Polytheism to Monotheism

Concepts of a God have evolved along with human society and in that process views that were once held to be valid have been abandoned, to be replaced by alternatives. Greek mythology gave us a huge pantheon of gods – abstract forms that were personified, such as the Titans and the familiar Olympian deities that included Aphrodite, Apollo, Hermes and Zeus, the sea and sky gods, agricultural deities and deified mortals. The biblical account of the God of Judaism, Christianity and Islam tells the story of a radical monotheism, of a God who displaced, for example, the gods of Babylonia and Sumer, who were believed to reside in their statues. Gradually, this Old Testament God unseated the polytheisms both of early Israel and of those countries through which the monotheism of biblical religion spread. In evolutionary terms, the success of monotheism is a cultural form of the 'survival of the fittest', that is, of a religion found to be fit for purpose in terms of what people considered relevant for a meaningful life and a cohesive society.

Fundamentalism remains a virulent force in most living world religions, but alongside this hard-edged trend there has also been a softer, modernizing tendency. The old personifications of monotheism have come to be understood by many in more abstract terms – expressed for example as the 'One', the 'Divine' or, in the words of the philosophical theologian Paul Tillich, the 'ground of our being'. In such terms as these, God is construed as a form of moral imagination or a life-force. In place of the intelligent designer some now envisage an eternal, omnipotent energy. This more abstract concept, of a divinity that in some way pervades our individual spirits or souls, accounts for the best of ourselves, and especially our capacity for selfless love. However, it is possible that human nature itself gave birth to such a belief, and that it is genetically programmed, a mechanism necessary for the survival of our species.

The kind of questions people have always asked relate to the origin of the universe and the life of this planet, the fact of suffering and death, the meaning and purpose of life, and whether or not life continues in some form after death. To ask such questions in the modern world is a very different undertaking than it was for the earliest groups of human beings. It is difficult for us to imagine having to use every moment of our waking life to ensure our physical survival in an environment that was constantly life-threatening, to secure a regular supply of food, adequate shelter and clothing, to keep the fire burning, and to protect the community from both marauding animals and enemies. If our lives were dependent on a migratory herd, then we would be nomadic, undertaking long and hazardous journeys. We would also have to deal with the problems of climate, especially of its extremes, the threat of drought or floods, earthquakes and volcanic eruption. Our lives would have been dominated by fear and anxiety caused by the unpredictability and uncertainty of life.

The first hunter-gathers were necessarily preoccupied with what it was that ensured fertility and determined the safe birth of animals and humans. They wondered about what controlled the wind, thunder, lightning, rain, the sudden and sometimes extreme changes of weather, and the more gradual movement through the seasons, and about what the power was that moved the lights they observed in the night sky. And, most importantly, they would have wanted to know if these powers were beneficent or malign, if they could be controlled, appeased, persuaded, harnessed to their advantage in the gruelling struggle to survive. When, in human evolution, our creative imagination developed, it radically transformed people's responses to the environment, from one of practical concern with what threatened and preserved life, to one of wonder and awe, the beginnings of a sense of 'something other'.

What we know of the beliefs, cults and religions of prehistory remains sketchy and is, of course, incomplete. The picture that has been put together from skeletons and artefacts found on the sites of settlements, permanent or otherwise, suggests a people who developed sufficient mental and physical skills to enable them to communicate with each other, to make tools, to hunt and to work together to ensure their survival. They were capable of reasoning and imagining, and both faculties were brought to bear on every aspect of their environment and the struggle to survive within it. Lost in the story of our social evolution are the names of those who discovered that instead of spending months following a migrating herd, or risking life in a dangerous hunt, animals could be captured, enclosed and domesticated, the earth tilled, seeds planted and crops cultivated. Once people lived in more settled communities, more considered thought could be given to the questions the struggle to survive demanded. The answers to these questions bore the seeds of the God-hypothesis.

Two concerns dominated the life of early humans: fertility and death. Both of these have kept us company down the centuries and they still preoccupy us. We can think of them as the factors that sustain and threaten life. The means of nurturing the former, and guarding against the latter have always been the stuff of which religion and a belief in God was made.

It is worth taking a closer look at i) fertility and the life-sustaining energies, and ii) the inevitability of death.

Fertility and the life-sustaining energies

Virtually all cultures developed fertility goddess cults, which are probably the earliest religions for which we have evidence in the form of artefacts and artwork. The belief in a goddess who governed reproductivity emerged as a natural response to a life based on animal husbandry and agriculture. Many of the cults and their goddesses have not survived, but a few have. Perhaps the most famous goddess of human fecundity is the Venus of Willendorf, a statuette discovered in Austria in 1908 by the Austro-Hungarian archaeologist Josef Szombathy. The figure, dating from approximately 23,000 BCE, represents what is now a fairly familiar image of a female fertility symbol, with large breasts, a heavy abdomen and a detailed vulva. We do not know exactly how such images were used, or if their worship required offerings or sacrifice; it is possible the images, believed to have potent influence, were just placed in the dwelling of a family wanting to reproduce.

In West Africa, the Ashanti still have an earth goddess of fertility called Asase Ya; in North America, Aztec mythology included Cihuacotl, the goddess of motherhood, fertility and midwives; in Europe, Celtic religion supported several goddesses, such as Damara, a fertility goddess who was worshipped in Britain. In Greek mythology, Priapus, of various parentage that included Aphrodite, Dionysus, Zeus, Pan or Hermes, was worshipped as a fertility god, and his responsibilities included the protection of livestock, fruit and plants, gardens and male genitalia. In frescos and statues, Priapus is shown with a large and permanent erection, which is both the source and brunt of ribald jokes. This provided some comic relief among the fertility cults that were otherwise taken very seriously. Aphrodite is Greek mythology's central fertility goddess; Robert Graves, in *The Greek Myths*, identified her as Priapus' mother. Venus was her Roman counterpart. Their cults practised ritual prostitution, as had other similar cults, for example, those of Sumeria, Akkadia, Babylon and Assyria.

The gods and goddesses of these fertility cults have long since been abandoned in mainstream Western culture, although the neo-pagan religion Wicca still retains an attachment to them. As a form of pantheism, the pagan, nature-worshipping Wicca tradition, which is associated with magic and witchcraft, supports belief in nature gods that sustain all life. Gerald Gardner, a Wiccan high priest and a polymath whose interests included anthropology, archaeology and the occult, was responsible for bringing Wicca to the notice of the public during the early 1950s. In *The Meaning of Witchcraft*, he wrote, 'The Gods are real, not as persons, but as vehicles of power.' Traditionally, however, these powers have been anthropomorphized, and in the next chapter we shall follow up the idea of person-ification, a practice characteristic of all religions both in their primitive and more sophisticated forms. Anthropo-morphism is a useful device, maybe even a necessary one, to accompany the hypothesis of gods or a God, since it makes contact and relationship more viable.

Fertility is only one example of what, in more general terms, we can think of as life-sustaining energies. The sun is another, and it has generated many powerful sun deity cults, aspects of which are found across many of the world's religions. Dante Alighieri wrote, 'There is no visible thing in all the world more worthy to serve as a type of God than the Sun; which illuminates with visible light itself first, and then all the celestial and elemental bodies.' In the *Rigveda* of Vedic Hinduism, the sun is identified with the god Surya, and the animating power of *atman*, the universal soul. Egyptian religion developed what was probably the most complete solar deity cult, centred on the sun god Ra, who was mostly associated with the sun in its mid-day phase, and whose image shows the god wearing the solar disk. As with the fertility goddesses, Ra had a varied portfolio; he was known also as Atum-Ra, the god of the setting sun, whose cult was centred at Heliopolis, the 'City of the Sun'. Ra was thought of as the source of life, the first being, and father of all the other gods and the pharaohs. Khepri or Khepera, depicted as a scarab beetle, was the god associated with the dawning or rising sun, and with rebirth. Known as the transformer, for example of night to day, Khepri was an aspect of both Ra and Atum. The Aztec sun god, Tonatiuh, had a more forbidding mythology. (In the Mexican language Nahuatl, *ollin Tonatiuh* means 'movement of the sun'.) Aztec cosmology was based on the concept of cyclic time and cosmic eras, each of which had its own sun god. Tonatiuh, known as 'the fifth sun', represents the current era. For this to continue, the sun god had to be kept moving through his cyclic journey across the sky and, to ensure this, it is thought thousands of human lives were offered to Tonatiuh in blood-sacrifice rituals.

Although the sun may be dominant among the major life-sustaining energies that have provided a source for concepts of god, rain and water have also given rise to deity-based cults in different parts of the world. However, in nature-based religions, most, if not all aspects of nature have been deified.

This is what lies behind animism (from the Latin *anima* – spirit, breath or soul), which is the attribution of a spirit to everything in nature, both animate and inanimate. The anthropologist Sir Edward Burnett Taylor considered animism to be 'a minimum definition of religion' and, with pantheism, it is certainly one of the sources of the God-hypothesis. Animism, however, implies the presence in everything of many different kinds of spirits, whereas pantheism usually refers to the indwelling of everything by the one spirit or God. Thus, in earlier societies, animism took the form of polytheism, which associated specific gods with particular forms of nature, for example rivers, glades, mountains, thunder, fire, the sea, the sky, the earth and so on. Gradually, polytheism gave ground to pantheism, a belief that the whole of nature, indeed, the entire universe, is a manifestation of the one God. Panentheism, a variation of this, suggests that God is greater than the sum total of nature, that rather than 'being' everything, God resides 'within' (*pan-en*) every aspect of nature.

Contemporary examples of animism are still to be found in African tribal religion, in Japan's Shintoism, in India's various Hindu traditions, in some Native American religions such as the beliefs of the Lakota Sioux, in neo-paganism, and some New Age cults. Nearly all the world's major religions, creationist or otherwise, have panentheistic elements. Pantheism is a characteristic of what are termed 'New Age' religions which draw on aspects of older religious teaching, together with the revival of cults such as Druidism and Wicca, and the more recent emergence of spiritual and religious groups rooted in Gaia philosophy.

Since the dominant concern of the earliest communities was to survive, it is unsurprising that their concepts of ultimate powers, that is of their gods, were related to whatever they believed sustained fertility and life, and ensured the kind of relationship with the natural world that enabled them to hunt, provide shelter, produce fire and so on.

The inevitability of death

The fact and fear of death, actually living with the knowledge of our mortality, is probably the most persistent source of the God-hypothesis. Knowing that life is temporary challenges, like nothing else, our understanding of its meaning and purpose. Thus, the mystery of dying and speculation about whether or not life, in some way, continues is the main drive behind humanity's impulse to religion. Every culture in the world has developed cults of the dead, centred on a final rite of passage. The earliest of these cults ameliorated the reality of death with belief in a life beyond the grave, which extended the process of living to the deceased. The belief that life continues through death gave greater force to the rituals and practices designed to facilitate the deceased's passage into the next life. Mother Earth was believed to be the source of life both for the living and the dead, which is why fertility figurines like the Venus of Willendorf have been found in all forms of mortuary settings. E O James, an anthropologist working in the field of comparative religion, said, 'it is not surprising . . . that the Goddess cult very early acquired a funerary and chthonian [underworld] significance when her domain was made to embrace the land of the dead'. James also made the important point that 'the earliest indications of the idea of immortality appear to have been associated with the head as the seat of the soul-substance and vitality'. It is, perhaps, for this reason that the cult of the skull became universal.

Separating the skull from the rest of the body is a very ancient practice. The custom dates from at least the early Palaeolithic period, approximately 2.7 million years to 200,000 years ago. Because of the food potential of the brain and bone marrow, cannibalism may provide all or part of the reason for the practice, but the anthropologist

Ian Kuijt and the Syrian archaeologist Youssef Kanjou tell us that skulls were prepared and arranged for worship long after death. In many parts of the world skulls were used in ancestor worship and the veneration of the dead, and the practice continues, for example, in some African tribal religions. Not only was it believed that the deceased enjoyed some form of continuity of life, but also that they could influence the fortunes of the living.

A pantheon of death-associated deities emerged as the death-cults developed. In Babylonia, Nergal presided over the underworld; ancient Egypt had Anubis and Osiris, gods related to mummification, the afterlife and the underworld; the Greeks had Thanatos and Hades; the Romans, Pluto; the Norse, Odin; the Yoruba, Iku; and the Celts, Morrigan. All of these are polytheistic religions. For Old Testament monotheism, the domain of the dead, variously termed Gehenna, Sheol or Hell, is given over to the Devil. In Judaism, the devil is not understood as an independent power in opposition to God. The Hebrew word, *ha-satan*, means 'the accuser', 'the adversary' or 'the obstacle', but while the term is rarely used in the Old Testament as a proper noun, its significance is ever-present, not as the source of evil, but as God's advocate who questions and tests his people. For example, in Job, Satan is referred to as one of 'the sons of God', or as an angel still on speaking terms with Yahweh. Similarly in Ezekiel. The theme is carried through into the New Testament where 'Satan' becomes the Devil traditionally identified with the rebellious fallen angel in the form of the tempting serpent of Eden. For example, Revelation 12:9 'And the great dragon was thrown down, that ancient serpent, who is called the Devil and Satan, the deceiver of the whole world.'

The mythologies and cults of the dead have changed their form, and the ancient gods are, for the most part, relegated to the history of religion and to imagery in museums, but our preoccupation with death, dying and the dead is as much part of daily living as ever it was. Perhaps the best-known celebration of death is the Mexican Day of the Dead, observed on 2 November, when families and friends come together to pray for those who have died. The rituals take place in the cemetery and the deceased's favourite foods and drinks are made available, photographs set up, toys provided for dead children, all actions contrived to encourage the return, to the place of burial, of the souls of the deceased, so that they will hear the prayers of the living and once more 'enjoy' their company. The Day of the Dead, of course, is now celebrated as the Roman Catholic All Souls' Day, and the Mexican observation draws heavily on the Christian tradition.

While to mourn and to celebrate the dead seems entirely natural, we use our own involvement in these rites as an affirmation of life in general and of our own life in particular. There is a sense in which each confrontation with death brings a feeling of relief, that in witnessing the death of another, we celebrate our own continuing life. The fear of death, the love of life, the natural feeling that we would rather be alive than dead, is one of the principal driving forces behind religion. In his Pulitzer Prize-winning book *The Denial of Death*, Ernest Becker argued that death is our most consuming anxiety, and that our fear of it is an inborn instinct we share with every animal. Fear of death alerts us to everything that is a risk to our life. However, as humans, we have an additional problem, what Becker calls our 'ambiguity': 'Man's anxiety is a function of his sheer ambiguity ... to be straightforwardly an animal or an angel. He cannot live heedless of his fate, nor can he take control over that fate and triumph over it by being outside the human condition.'

Although it is not the point that Becker is making, we can see for ourselves how the fear of death has led to the

God-hypothesis, since it gives to God the power and control over both life *and* death, a control that we ourselves lack, but which we can harness by faith. In Chapter 7, we will look more closely at the whole issue of death and survival, questioning, and going beyond Paul's clear affirmation of faith in 1 Corinthians 15: 55–56. 'O, death, where is thy victory? O, death, where is thy sting?'

The gods of death that demanded human sacrifice as the price for sustaining life-giving energies have, long since, been relegated to history and, with a few notable exceptions found in the revival of primitive animisms, for example Celtic and Norse traditions, so have the nature gods. In Western culture we no longer worship the sun, the moon, the rain, trees and mountains, the concept of polytheism having given way long ago to a vigorous monotheism. The concepts of God in the major world religions have survived, because their function, usefulness, power and relevance are still found to be fit for purpose. Especially in the developing world, where life remains subject to increasingly extreme changes of climate, where drought can put a generation at risk, the God-idea continues to offer both an explanation of these natural, elemental threats, and the hope of over-coming them. However, the numerous gods of death are generally no longer found to be useful, and have been banished to their own netherworlds, taking their cults along with them. Nevertheless, we have noted how death remains a central issue in life, and as such continues to sustain the idea of a God who is all-loving, and who offers the 'hope of a life to come'.

Among the world's major religions, Buddhism alone teaches that the problem of human existence is not death, but life itself. Its pleasures, joys and satisfactions notwith-standing, life is suffering. Furthermore, the Buddhist belief in reincarnation teaches that we are caught up in an endless cycle of lives. The attainment of enlightenment, becoming a *buddha*, is the means of breaking out of *samsara*, or the cycle of birth, death and rebirth. The goal of Buddhist philosophy is not to overcome death and receive eternal life, but to end the cycle of reincarnation. Buddhism is non-theistic, and because there is no God-hypothesis there exists a different kind of metaphysics, one based on realization rather than revelation, which encourages practitioners to look within themselves for an experience of unity with everything that is beyond them.

The essentially Judeo-Christian concept of biblical monotheism, however, pivots around the notion that death is 'the last enemy', and one to be vanquished. The meaning of life is therefore cast in terms of combative dualisms, life against death, matter against spirit, evil against good. Here, the hypothesis is of a creator God, the originator and sustainer of the universe and the life it supports, but who, in any real terms, has no answer to death. Death is something that was not part of the original scheme of things but which, according to the book of Genesis, was introduced as a consequence of the first man and woman disobeying God's instructions. In the biblical context, the hypothesis is of a God whose original creation was perfect, and in which death had no part. That it was introduced as the punishment for the sin of disobedience served to set up a salvational process leading to a 'new creation', which although still dominated by death, offers a solution to its threat. All this can be inferred from the account of creation in Genesis, the most familiar of all biblical stories.

Monotheism has made a crucial contribution to the God-hypothesis. The concept of just one God became more accessible, even more comprehensible, when Christianity added to it the attribute of incarnation, that is Jesus as the embodiment of God as his Son. The hypothesis has moved from the polytheisms of remote, impersonal powers, to a form of monotheism that renders God as a person, a deity with whom one can have a relationship. This returns us to the idea of anthropomorphism, especially with regard to the language used in the Bible and elsewhere, that overlays an abstract idea with inter-personal terms of reference, with what the German philosopher Martin Buber, for example, termed the 'I–Thou' relationship. The God of the Bible has evolved from one who is remote, to one with whom it is possible to be intimate. In this form, the concept of God has had a long and flourishing history; it has survived every kind of opposition and persecution in an increasingly secularized society, because of the 'need' we have for relationship. This fundamental human necessity, to anchor the abstract notion of God in an immediate and personal encounter, has generated as much energy for the God-hypothesis as did the earlier identification of God with natural forces.

What continues to cause problems for the relational form of the God-hypothesis is the tension between personalism and universalism. To be fit for purpose, a concept of God must now be of a kind that is accessible to everyone, not only to a 'chosen' few who are able to subscribe to creedal and theological statements. It must be capable of being relevant to the complex demands of everyday life, while also accountable for the origin and maintenance of the universe. The debate about the existence of the traditional concept of God (the omnipotent, omniscient creator) is currently taking place because, under criticism from both old and new atheism, and from modern philosophical theology, the received tradition is coming apart at the seams.

From the foregoing, we can reasonably conclude that human beings have always had the need to believe in something other than themselves, but in a way that fosters an understanding of the nature and meaning of life. Until relatively recently, this need to believe and understand has been determined by the struggle to survive physically, and it remains so in the world's poorer countries. In the West, most of us are fortunate in being able to take our immediate survival for granted. The life-sustaining necessities are delegated to those who produce and distribute food, to the medical services and to the armed forces. Even so, a belief in God lingers so persistently and universally that we must consider if it is somehow built into our make-up, and indispensable to our survival. Even if, nowadays, the God-hypothesis is determined by our culture and upbringing, or by social pressures and influences, it is possible that at the deepest level there is a basic psychic need at work. Did primitive man read into nature a metaphysics that enabled him to feel 'at home' in the universe, or did he bring to nature a metaphysics born of his own intuition? Was the God-hypothesis invented as an explanation, or disclosed as a perception? These are questions that will be taken up in subsequent chapters.

It needs to be said that in addition to the major living religions of the world there are innumerable minor ones, such as the Baha'i faith, Native American religions, Rastafarianism , Jainism, Jehovah's Witnesses and the New Age cults, for whom God remains a vibrant and relevant energy. Beyond all forms of organized religion, there are countless individuals for whom faith in the existence of God thrives in a more subjective manner.

Our preoccupation with death and survival, and with trying to understanding the meaning of life, are not only the concerns of traditional religious theology, and a distinction can be made between, say, a creed or theology and an ideology or philosophy. There are, as we shall see, various systems of thought that provide a ground for understanding who we are and why we are here, and which offer a rational explanation for the fact of death. If these systems of thought were to be formalized by society they might fulfil the same purpose as traditional religion by providing an understanding of the meaning and purpose of human life in terms of a socio-politico-legal system and of good government, together with models for aesthetics and morality. Some of these philosophies, for example Plato's concept of 'the Republic' and the philosopher-king, and Thomas More's model island, Utopia, with its seemingly communal society, point to the creation of an ideal or perfected society.

It is useful now to look at some examples, across time and culture, of what can be thought of as the God of the philosophers to see if, like the various forms of gods and God already discussed, one or more might offer a relevant and viable contribution.

2. The God of the Philosophers

China's Taoism (or Daoism), like Buddhism, is non-theistic. Considered by some to be a religion, Taoism is really a philosophical system, but one that is applicable to the administration and government of society and to the daily life of the individual. Its principal thinkers were Laozi (Lao Tzu, *c*. 6th century BCE) and Zhuangzi (Chuang Tzu, *c*. 4th century BCE). The Tao is an all-embracing first cause from which everything arises and to which everything returns. Its central themes include virtue, morality and ethics, and an enquiry into the nature and meaning of life and death. Preserving and prolonging life is basic to Taoist teaching, with clear implications for medicine, self-defence and concern for human welfare. *Tao*, or *dao*, 'the Way', is the primordial source of order, the origin of the appearances of all things, the 'unproduced producer', which is also the guarantor of the stability of everything that exists. The philosophy focuses on *te*, or *de*, 'virtuosity', or the power for the good, that is aesthetic excellence rather than morality; the power, the essential energy of *dao*, relates to one's ability to execute one's *dao* correctly. *Te* gives to everything the character that defines it, and the means of practising it is called *wu wei,* 'non-doing'; Laozi taught that, 'by letting go it all gets done. The world is won by those who let it go. But when you try and try, the world is beyond the winning.' Doing by not doing is a seeming contradiction, and for the Western mind a paradox. It requires non-intervention in the natural course of events, but at the same time spontaneous action, which, because it lacks premeditated purpose, or what we might call 'intention', is entirely appropriate. The capacity simply to accept the way things are is one of the keys to right living, as Zhuangzi pointed out: 'Flow with whatever may happen and let your mind be free. Stay centred by accepting whatever you are doing. This is the ultimate.' Interestingly, *wu wei* can also be described as patterns of organic energy or matter, and it is used in this way by writers such as Gary Zukav and Ken Wilbur in connection with quantum theory and the new physics.

The hypothesis here is not of a God in the traditional biblical sense, but of the existence of what might be termed a 'life-force', known in Chinese thought as *chi,* literally 'air' or 'breath'. This is understood as a free-flowing force that, while being impersonal and thus without personifications, is something shared by all forms of life, and with which the individual can connect. In so doing such a person can become wise and cultivated, a model citizen, who through the esoteric quest to cultivate the primordial breath, or *chi,* is potentially immortal.

A very different and more analytic view is given by Plotinus (*c.* 204/5–270 CE) who was one of the principal interpreters of Plato. He was born in Egypt and educated in Alexandria. His philosophical system is built around three realities, what he termed *hypostases* – 'soul', 'mind', and 'the One' or 'the Good'. He takes from Plato the idea that everything we see is a relative expression of its absolute form. That is, that behind every material entity, that with which our senses are engaged, there exists a non-material, abstract, counterpart. It is these that represent fundamental reality, not the material world of change. Soul is concerned with discursive thought, mind with intuition, and the One or the Good with highest mystical awareness. Reality is elusive, a series of reflections that become increasingly fragmented, originating with the One, then passing to the mind and the soul. The One, being the source of everything that exists, is therefore, by definition, good. Because of the process of fragmentation, the mind is only a minute part, or emanation, of the One, and the purpose of life is for the mind to return to its source. Plotinus said, 'I am striving to give back the Divine in myself to the Divine in the All.' What we are, and what we become, depends on our own participation in this process. Because the One exists in all of its innumerable fragments, the observable world represents 'unity in diversity', but the soul, contemplating this, moves all the time between the fragmentary objects it observes, unaware of their inherent unity. Plotinus put it this way: 'God is not external to anyone, but is present with all things, though they are ignorant that he is so.'

Plotinus is particularly interested in beauty. He says, 'Being is desirable because it is identical with Beauty, and Beauty is loved because it is Being.' Morality and aesthetics are derived from this principle, and all should strive to attain beauty. 'Withdraw into yourself and look,' advises Plotinus. 'And if you do not find yourself beautiful yet, act as does the creator of a statue that is to be made beautiful: he cuts away here, he smooths there, he makes this line lighter, this other purer, until a lovely face has grown from his work. So do you also: cut away all that is excessive, straighten all that is crooked, bring light to all that is overcast, labour to make all one glow of beauty and never cease chiselling your statue, until there shall shine out on you from it the godlike splendour of virtue, until you see the perfect goodness surely established in the stainless shrine' (*Enneads*, 1.6.9). Society and its government are to be managed on the same principle; the world in its entirety is to be beautified.

Plotinus' hypothesis is entirely abstract. He clearly wants to account for the origin of life and the universe, and he does so with the entity he calls the One. His God is impersonal, having neither name nor personality. It is not clear if the One actually created the universe; we get the sense only of the universe and all forms of life being fragmentations of an original unity. This is not a God with whom we can have a relationship, nor is it a God we could worship beyond a general feeling of gratitude for the life we have, which is a minute part of the life of the whole. Little is said about whether the One is a source of strength and comfort, and beyond a clear but general appeal to the concept of beauty, no guidance is given as to how we should order our society or conduct our individual lives. With a vague notion that death will return us to the life of the whole, we are left to aspire to the ideal as best we can.

More than a millennium later, in northern Europe, Baruch Spinoza broke away from the dominant tradition of Western theism to produce an original contribution to philosophy based on logic and deduction, a method associated with 17th-century Enlightenment scientists and astronomers, such as Descartes, Newton, Galileo and Kepler. Spinoza's main interest was ethics: he wanted to establish what is good, and what works best for human beings. His thinking is based on the belief that all explanations of anything are deductive, that to understand anything we need to be able to show, by means of axioms, a conclusion based on logical necessity. His argument is retrogressive, taking us back from truths about human nature to the truth about an absolute and infinite being whose existence he took to be a logical necessity. Spinoza reasoned, 'that the eternal and infinite being we call God, or Nature, acts from the same necessity from which he exists'. This infinite being is so radically different from the biblical God that, in 1656, Spinoza was expelled from the Jewish community and excommunicated from the synagogue. He built his philosophical system on a concept of universal substance, or one reality, that combined the physical and mental worlds, thus reversing Descartes's body–mind dualism. In reaching for the concept of a universal substance, Spinoza made no distinction between God and nature, saying they are just two names for the same reality. For this reason he is considered, by some, to be a pantheist.

Because logical necessity lay at the heart of his method, Spinoza was a determinist, since everything that happens does so because it must. He insisted, 'Nothing in the universe is contingent, but all things are conditioned to exist and operate in a particular manner by the necessity of the divine nature.' This raises, of course, the extent to which human beings are free, and freedom is something Spinoza concedes to some, but not all people. He claimed that, 'He alone is free who lives with free consent under the entire guidance of reason.' Emotions and passions play a large part in the attainment of freedom – 'men are conscious of their own desires, but are ignorant of the causes whereby that desire has been determined'; the person who is free will be one who is rational, not just intellectually, but someone who by reason has mastered his passions. Doing so will lead to virtue and happiness. (See Chapter 7 for a discussion of free will and determinism.)

Spinoza has reasoned his way to a concept of God that is not in any way personal, nor the agent of creation, but one difficult to distinguish from the natural world. 'God', he asserts, 'is the indwelling and not the transient cause of all things.' Life and the universe are controlled by cause and effect, by every event being consequent on the previous one. What guides us, essentially, is natural law – and since God cannot be outside of nature, this law is synonymous with the will of God. In the Preface to Part IV of his *Ethics*, Spinoza summed up his conception of God thus, 'By God I understand a being absolutely infinite, that is, a substance consisting of an infinity of attributes, of which each one expresses an eternal and infinite essence.'

In Germany a century or so later, Georg Hegel's dominant interest was history, and the history of thought; he regarded previous philosophies as necessary stages in the development of thought, perception and language. Even though it is important for our discussion, we cannot here go too deeply into Hegel's system, which is vast and complex. (See Chapter 3, 'Arguments from History'.) It is useful, however, to glance at it here in passing, because Hegel shares with his influential part-contemporary Immanuel Kant a desire to find out how we can be sure that what we know is true. This is a theme that will recur thought this book. Like Kant, Hegel was concerned with truths, but not truths that are necessary in terms of formal logic. Kant's main concern was with what he termed 'necessary truths', of the kind associated with the natural sciences. What we know to be true cannot be entirely objective since our mind is not passive in its relationship to objects or facts, but contributes to them what we already know and have experienced. He adopted the view that everything that exists must be mental, a view that has come to be known as Idealism. Put in other words, Idealism maintains that experience is ultimately based on mental activity, a view that contrasts completely with Realism, which asserts that reality is independent of our perceptions and conceptual schemes, beliefs, and so on.

Hegel's view of the world contributes an important question to the debate with which this book is concerned. The problem posed is, if everything is in the mind, as Hegel asserts, how can we distinguish between the subjective and the objective, the true from the false? This led Hegel to what is called the 'coherence theory of truth', which, simply put, argues that truth is 'system' – we can know whether or not something is true by the extent to which it contributes to a single and complete system of thought. If any proposition advances that cause, then it must be true. However, we may need to wait before finding out if the proposition does contribute to the cause, thus things can be partly true or partly false. What Hegel is engaging us in, therefore, is a process, and one that for him operates entirely through history.

What kind of God-hypothesis emerges from Hegel's system of thought? Instead of the German word for God, he uses *geist*, which can mean 'mind' or 'spirit'. Developing the idea of *geist*, he uses phrases such as 'universal mind', 'universal force' and 'universal will'. In the Jena Lectures of 1805–6, he said, 'The activity of the universal is unity. The universal will has to gather itself into this unity. It has first to constitute itself as universal will, out of the will of individuals.' God, or the supreme mind, is a collective; it is both a combination of individual wills and an original, independent resource. 'The universal will is prior to them [individual wills], it is absolutely there for them – they are in no way immediately the same.' Hegel searched for a 'universal' that would integrate everything with which history and its processes are concerned: the relationship of mind to nature, subjective and objective knowledge, psychology, and the state, together with its art, religion and philosophy. In focusing on 'mind' and 'will' he allowed the perennial contradictions, such as freedom and determinism, immanence and transcendence, to exist together. This concept of God, or *geist*, is primarily intellectual, a God considered as an eternal 'idea', and one that points to a future philosophical view we know as Existentialism.

This discussion of the God-hypothesis, its origins and evolution, has moved from the primitive polytheistic animisms of early human beings to what might be termed the God of the philosophers. Between these, originating and developing along the way, are the more familiar views of God represented by the traditions of the major world religions. Those concepts of God offered by ideologies and philosophies seem to lack vitality and staying power; they do not have the kind of energy possessed by a world religion. We cannot imagine Hegel's 'universal mind' or Spinoza's 'absolutely infinite being' becoming the basis of a new religion. Why this is so, is a question that will be discussed in a later chapter.

In summary, we can say that the traditional Western view of God is derived from the Bible and the Quran. From these we understand God to have always existed, to be eternal, spirit, the creator and sustainer of everything. Judaism knows him as Yahweh, the 'One who Is', Elohim, 'the Name', and Adonai, 'the Lord'. Christianity refers to him as the Father, Son and Holy Spirit, the Lord, King of Kings, and the Almighty. In Islam there are 99 names for Allah, among them, Al-Awwal, 'The First', Al-Akhir, 'The Last', and As-Samad, 'The Eternal.' Eastern concepts are varied: Hinduism's different forms include polytheism, mono-theism and henotheism (the worship of just one god while accepting the existence of others); Buddhism, however, is non-theistic and thus not founded on a belief in a God or gods. Because it is the sustainer of life on Earth, there was a time when people believed that the sun was God, or the principal god among many. Other natural objects worshipped as gods included the moon, mountains, trees and the personified energies of the awe-inspiring forces of nature. Among polytheistic religions it was usual for one powerful god to dominate the others: for example, the sun god Ra, whose cult made him the chief of the cosmic deities in ancient Egypt, or Zeus as the spiritual father of ancient Greece's Olympian hierarchy, and Brahman, the supreme being of Hinduism. The hypothesis with which the debate is mainly concerned is the biblical God, and it is the passionately held arguments for and against the existence of this God that are the main interest of this book.

Over the millennia our concepts of God have radically changed. In the course of this process what the word 'God' represented evolved from notions of primitive polytheism, through traditional biblical monotheism, to a belief in something entirely abstract and ineffable. Whatever view believers now hold about God is maintained against a rigorous atheism in a society that is thoroughly secularized and marked by a culture shaped by science and technology rather than by theology and doctrine. We can study phenomena macrocosmically and microscopically to the point of formulating a plausible, but not yet complete, theory of everything. This culture is one that is quickly becoming global and, as we shall see, it asks new and challenging questions about the form and nature of any God that might exist.

Chapter Two

What or Who is God?

BEHIND ALL THE IDEAS ABOUT GOD lie assumptions as to what a god, or God is. The debate is about the existence of such a being, but who, or what is being debated? To ask what the word 'God' stands for is to pose a question that has been pondered since the beginning of history. This is not just a theoretical question about etymology and original meaning, more importantly it is a question about the nature and use of language. Whether or not God is a 'who' or a 'what', we need to consider not God, but the 'notion' of God, a distinction the philosopher Mark Taylor makes between concept and category. 'Is God,' he asks, in his book *About Religion*, 'that which eludes concept-ualisation and categorisation? Might "God" be the name for that "in" language that does not belong to language, the name . . . for that which language can never name or cannot avoid naming the unnameable?' Soren Kierkegaard held the view that 'God' cannot be either conceptualized or categorized, which is why he referred to God as 'the absolutely different'. Perhaps, for this reason, Taylor suggested that 'God is a pseudonym'. Atheists and theists alike assume the pseudonym to be the real, or actual name, but if what is taken to be the real name is false, what does the pseudonym stand for? In broad terms we are left with the category of the sacred, the 'other', and those various abstract phrases mentioned in the previous chapter such as 'the ground of being'. What we are concerned with is the scrabble of language to say something meaningful about a concept that in Kierkegaard's thinking is 'an infinite and qualitative difference'.

The problem philosophers and theologians have always had to face is that even the term 'concept' is inadequate in reference to God. How can language be used for something that is beyond conceptualization? Perhaps, for this reason, the most elegant statements about God have been made by music or possibly painting, art forms that aspire to the necessary degree of abstraction in order to 'say', or disclose something of meaning.

The possible origins of the God-hypothesis have been discussed, but what can be said of the origin of the word 'God' and what it represents? The terms, 'Yahweh', or 'Ar-Rahmaan', one of Islam's 99 names for 'Allah', are examples of words or names by which God is known. There is no clear derivation for the word 'God' itself, and thus, no clear meaning. Joseph McCabe, a free-thinking rationalist, suggested the word's origin was from the old High German *gott*. The Icelandic *gu* is a close homophone of the Sanskrit *hu*, which means 'to call upon' or 'invoke'. The old Teutonic form *gudo* meant that which was invoked or worshipped by sacrifice, it carried a neuter gender, but became masculine, it is thought, due to the Christian use of the word. The familiar English form 'God' entered the language via Anglo-Saxon. It is beyond the scope of this discussion to carry the search for the origin of the word back into Hebrew, Aramaic, Greek and Latin.

In any language, the words used as names for God, such as those given toward the end of the previous chapter, tell us more about the attributes of God, that is the traditional characteristics like omnipotence, than the etymological origin of the term. All the languages of the world, both living and dead, have their traditional word for God, and while it may not be possible to know exactly what they meant originally, we know, at least in general terms, something of the concept they represent today.

The word, with its associated meanings, has gradually acquired a bad reputation and, despite its elusive etymology, there is a problem with 'God'. In his poignantly titled book *The Eclipse of God*, Martin Buber tells of being asked by a friend he was visiting how he could continue to use the word 'God' since no one would understand the word as he intended it to be used, since it is beyond all comprehension and conceptualization. 'All the innocent blood that has been shed for it has robbed it of its radiance,' his friend continued, 'all the injustice covering it has effaced its features. When I hear the highest called "God", it sometimes seems almost blasphemous.' Buber replied by saying that the word was the most heavily laden of all, the most soiled and mutilated. He said, 'Just for this reason I may not abandon it . . . we cannot cleanse the word "God" and we cannot make it whole; but, defiled and mutilated as it is, we can raise it from the ground and set it over an hour of great care.'

The reputation of the word 'God' does not seem to have improved since Nietzsche pronounced that 'God is Dead'. *The Eclipse of God* was published in the early 1950s and, if anything, God's standing has dropped even lower. While in Europe and North America the majority still have some idea of what the term 'God' represents, the demography of belief indicates a marked trend to atheism or agnosticism. The reasons for this are not complicated: secular ideologies and the influences of science, especially the new physics and evolutionary biology, have not only undermined faith in the concept of God, but have offered an alternative, avowedly rational world-view. What has been abandoned are the traditional biblical notions of what God is, and to understand the ground of the debate, its terms of reference, it is useful to look at the conventional ideas more fully.

The arguments for and against the existence of God will be fully discussed in the following chapters; the point here is to have a clear idea of what is being debated by looking at the traditional sense in which the word God is used. Any definition of God will be composite; it will be made up of several layers of meaning. Because it is primarily the biblical concept of God that is under scrutiny by the New Atheists and is defended by contemporary theists, the discussion, for the moment, will focus on the received concepts of God that have radically influenced the history of Western thought and culture.

Firstly, St John's gospel, 4:24, states, 'God is spirit.' This takes us immediately into the realm of metaphysics and therefore directly to the problem at the heart of this debate. Metaphysics, from the Greek, *meta ta physika,* meaning 'after the things of nature', is a philosophical discipline that enquires into realities claimed to exist beyond human sense-perception. To what extent can we call anything real, or true, that contravenes the laws of science? The purpose is not to argue the point here, but to explain it. To try and understand what the word 'God' represents has nothing to do with demonstrating whether or not such a being exists. The concept that God is spirit is saying that *if* such a being as God does exist, then it does so without material form or substance and thus is 'beyond' the world of experience.

While the natural sciences are concerned to understand what existence means to particular parts or aspects of the world and the universe, metaphysics is a branch of philosophy concerned with describing existence, or reality, as a whole. It has given rise to a subject discipline with its own characteristic arguments about the existence of anything said to be suprasensible, arguments that will recur throughout this book. However, a comprehensive agenda of metaphysics will have a particular application to the subject of God. Because it is concerned with the suprasensible, metaphysics sets out to demonstrate the existence of something that is beyond the terms of reference of our present state of scientific knowledge. It is assumed that we are incapable of establishing as fact anything that is beyond the scope of our sense experience, and it is this assertion that believers in God reject. By stating a belief in a God that is spirit, the believer is asserting an experience that has nothing whatsoever to do with those areas of knowledge that are defined by natural law. The main problem with this is its subjectivity, that the truth or otherwise contained in the belief cannot be established for anyone other than the believer. In this respect, even though there are many who would recognize the claim and confess to having experienced 'the same thing', the theists have a monopoly of that particular truth, since whatever validates it is based on these subjective perceptions and experiences. Because such statements cannot be supported in the usual way, they are dismissed by rational thinkers, not as being either true or false, but as meaningless.

We can, however, look at the statement 'God is spirit' in another way. Instead of regarding it as an affirmation of a reality that cannot be proved, we can regard it as an illustration of the way we think about reality. Ever since Kant's *Prolegomena to All Future Metaphysics*, philosophy has upheld the notion that the proper way to understand metaphysics is not by an enquiry into the accepted idea of reality, but by examining the structure of our thinking *about* reality, that is the way we think about what reality is. Kant's conceptual framework was fixed, but other philosophers disagreed. For example, R G Collingwood, who was interested in the philosophy of history, suggested in his 1940 *Essay on Metaphysics* that any conceptual framework, rather than being fixed, simply explained the underlying thoughts of its own period. If this is true, we have to allow for the conceptual framework to change through various periods and across different cultures. Thus, to say 'God is spirit' at the onset of the 21st century has a very different conceptual context than it did, for example, in the 1st, 14th, 16th or 18th centuries. 'God is Spirit' remains a metaphysical assertion but the physics it transcends is of a very different order and, as we shall see, any attempts to validate or disprove the belief 'God is Spirit' will also need a new conceptual framework.

The second, traditional definition of God is to be found in the First Letter of John, 4:8, which tells us 'God is Love'. The idea of love, it can safely be assumed, is easier to understand and is more accessible than the idea of spirit, but in this case, while the assertion retains a metaphysical aspect, the emotion of love, the feeling of profound affection or romantic or sexual attachment, exists without recourse to the belief that God is love, or that God exists at all. The author of the letter had hoped to clarify the concept of God, both to heighten it and to root it in everyone's experience, by attaching it to a feeling or emotion every living person would understand. John exhorts us to 'love one another', because, 'he who loves is born of God and knows God. He who does not love does not know God', *because* 'God is love.' Even though, in 1 Corinthians 13, Paul assures us that of the three abiding qualities, faith, hope and love, love is the greatest, to state that God *is* love, does not offer proof of God.

In some ways the word 'love' has similar problems to the word 'God', and this does not really need explaining beyond pointing out the extent to which it is also misused and abused, and the wide of range of meaning associated with it. The Bible, the principal source of Western culture's concept of God, has countless references to love broadly cast in three ways, God's love of us, our love of God, and our love for each other. Love of God is thought to be close to, or the same as, knowledge of God. In his book *Ethics of*

Pure Will, the Neo-Kantian philosopher Hermann Cohen wrote, 'The more the knowledge of God is simultaneously felt to be love of God, the more passionate becomes the battle for faith, the struggle for the knowledge of God and for the love of God.' Cohen is saying that if by our love (something we all experience and understand) we can gain an unassailable knowledge of God, then to love must become the driving passion of our lives. Cohen is responding to his debt to Kant, for whom God was just an idea, a supposition Cohen shared, but he also wanted to get beyond the mere idea, to true knowledge. He argued that, 'If I love God, then I no longer *think* [italics added] Him, since by means of the love, the idea, the abstract concept, becomes knowledge.' Finally, Cohen states that, 'the love of God exceeds all knowledge . . . A man's consciousness is completely filled when he loves God. This knowledge, which absorbs all others, is no longer merely knowledge, but love.' The process is cyclic: if God is love, then by loving we can know God. The knowledge, however, is so complete, so expulsive of everything else, that the knowing itself becomes love. It is not always easy to make a distinction between knowing someone and loving them; in our closest and most abiding relationships, the knowledge is the love, and the love is the knowledge.

Perhaps it was for this reason that the Bible commanded love. Simply put, love is useful, it is pragmatic. In John 3:16, the writer declares that, 'God so loved the world, that he gave his only Son . . .' Jesus's commandment to 'love one another' was a means to the end of binding the early Christian community together in the face of severe persecution. Jesus added a commandment to the original ten Moses received at Sinai, 'a new commandment I give you, that you love one another' (John 13:34). The model for this was Jesus' love for his disciples, 'even as I have loved you'. But the author of the gospel would have known that love cannot be commanded, that we are simply not capable of loving everyone, even though that is encouraged to the point of loving our enemies, those who castigate and traduce us. Most of us find it impossible to love the stranger, even the concept, the idealism of it, we find hard to grasp. We even find it difficult to love our neighbour who is, traditionally, the person suggested, and there are times when loving those closest to us is put under strain; even loving ourselves can sometimes be a confused and uneasy affair. The Bible also exhorts us to love God, 'and you shall love the Lord your God, with all your heart and all you soul and all your might' (Deuteronomy 6:5).

How does this notion that God is love, fit into the debate about God's existence? Clearly, the love and the act of loving do not require the God-hypothesis: we can love fully and faithfully without believing that God is love; we can be loved without any necessity to believe God exists. Love does not, in itself, constitute a proof of God's existence, but it changes the ground of the debate in that the love of anything rests in actual relationship. These are themes that will taken up again. (See Chapter 7.6.)

Thirdly, the First Letter of John, 1:15, says that, 'God is light.' In John's gospel, 8:12, Jesus says to his disciples, 'I am the light of the world,' and this is repeated in John 9:5 as part of an account of Jesus restoring sight to a blind man. This is a token of his being the source of light for all humanity. The symbolism here, of course, is obvious. The assertion that God is light is in the form of a metaphor, that is, while the claim that 'God is spirit' and 'God is love' is meant to be taken literally, that 'God is light' is entirely symbolic, an idea which, in principle, is shared by many religions. The metaphor carries with it two important concepts for the claim that God exists: one is the concept of revelation, the other is the concept of realization. These subjects will be further developed in Chapter 5, which discusses the variety and nature of religious experience; for the present it is enough to note that revelation implies a 'revealer', that such knowledge as is given comes from without. Realization, in contrast, suggests that all necessary knowledge is already contained within our minds, we have only to recognize it, to 'see the light'. Both concepts can be said to be forms of enlightenment.

The metaphor, however, contributes to our understanding of one important aspect of the debate about the existence of God, that it is also a debate about theories of knowledge, about how we get to know what we know, and about how we can be sure that what we know is valid. The claim that God is light, in an enlightenment sense, is also a claim that God is knowledge of a particular kind, derived in a particular way. The New Testament sources quoted above speak of both light and darkness which, to follow the metaphor through, is about knowledge and ignorance, and although we are concerned with biblical religion, it is a distinction Buddhists in particular would understand in ultimate terms. The background to the metaphor is to be found in the Old Testament; in Genesis, darkness preceded creation and represented chaos and emptiness, light, the beginning of creation. 'Darkness was on the face of the deep ... and God said, "Let there be light," and there was light' (Genesis 1:2–3). The theme runs throughout the Old Testament, for example: 'The Lord is my light and my salvation' (Psalm 27:1); 'For the commandment is a lamp and the teaching a light' (Proverbs 6:23); and 'the Lord will be your everlasting light, and God will be your glory' (Isaiah 60:19). In the Kabbalah, the ancient tradition of Jewish mysticism *Aur*, light, is a singularity of infinite energy, or limitless light.

All of the preceding is intended to illustrate the range of meaning in the concept 'God is light', not to authenticate it. Light is a powerful and, as shown, an ancient metaphor, but it is also a creative energy, and as such it is understood not merely as an attribute of God, but as a synonym for God.

God is spirit, God is love, God is light. Fourthly, we need to add, 'God is Word'. The idea stands apart from the others and brings a new dimension to the discussion. The biblical texts have made clear that whatever is meant by God was there at the beginning. 'In the beginning God . . .' and God in the beginning 'created the heavens and the earth' (Genesis 1:1). This is the foundation of the creationist creed, and it turns up in another form in the famous prologue to John's gospel: 'In the beginning was the Word, and the Word was with God, and the Word was God' (John 1:1). This is part of what philosophers know as the *logos* doctrine. The Greek term *logos* can mean 'word', 'speech' or 'reason.' Aristotle applied the term to what he called, 'reasoned discourse'. The 'Word', has been taken by various commentators to mean, wisdom, or the common law of nature that maintains the unity of the universe, or the agent of creation which may, or may not, be divine. Through the influence of the Hellenistic Jewish philosopher, Philo of Alexandria, the *logos* became identified with God's creative principle, that is the urge, or energy to create. The author of John's gospel also identifies the 'Word' with God's incarnation as Jesus of Nazareth, 'the Word became flesh and made his dwelling among us' (John 1:14).

However, the range of the meaning of *logos* is wider than the Christian concept of it. In his commentary on John's gospel, the New Testament scholar G R Beasley-Murray wrote, 'What we have in the prologue is a coming together of notions buried deep in the cultures of East and West', and it is this syncretism that has continued down the years. In the Sufi philosophy of Ibn Arabi the *logos* is 'Universal Man', a mediating link between people and the divine. In his system of analytical psychology, Jung used the term *logos* for the rational, critical faculty. In *Psychology of Religion East and West* he writes, 'the wisdom of God was often identified with the cosmogenic Logos'. In the wisdom literature of the Old Testament, God's wisdom is personified as female. The Book of Proverbs, for example, assures us that, 'Happy is the man who finds wisdom . . . she is more precious than jewels and nothing you desire can compare with her' (Proverbs 3:13 & 15), and Wisdom describes herself as the *logos*, the Word of God, 'For the Lord giveth wisdom; from his mouth comes knowledge and understanding' (Proverbs 2:6). With this wise, rational faculty of the *logos*, Jung contrasted the emotional, mythical faculty he termed *mythos*, the Greek word meaning a story, or legend. The opposition here is between the rational and the irrational, and it sets the tension in which the debate about the existence of God takes place.

One further, important, point needs to be made about the idea of the *logos* and the statement, 'God is Word'. If this is any way true, what kind of 'word' is it? Is the 'Word', a noun, an adjective, a verb, a noun-verb, an adjectival noun?

Encouraged by Pope Pius XII, a French translation of the original Hebrew and Greek of the Bible was made by the Roman Catholic École Biblique in Jerusalem. It was published in 1956 as the Jerusalem Bible. It translated the opening verse of John's gospel in this way, '*Au commencement était le Verbe et le Verbe était avec Dieu et le Verbe était Dieu,*' and verse 9 as, '*Le Verbe était la lumière véritable, qui éclaire tout homme; il venait dans le monde,*' and verse 14, '*Et le Verbe s'est fait chair et il a habité parmi nous.*' The usual French translation of 'word', as '*mot*' or '*parole*', has become, '*verbe*'.

In his book *The Mystical Kabbalah*, Rabbi David Cooper writes, 'God is not a noun, but a verb.' Richard

Buckminster Fuller, the American designer famous for his geodesic domes, wrote a poem called 'God is Verb', in which he stated, 'Here is God's purpose, God to me, it seems, is a verb not a noun,' and he said the same thing of himself in his book *I Seem To Be a Verb*, 'I live on Earth at the present, and I don't know what I am. I know I'm not a category. I am not a thing – noun. I seem to be a verb, an evolutionary process – an integral function of the universe.' Nor is God a noun for native Americans. Dan Moonhawk Alford, a Cheyenne Indian linguist and teacher, put it like this, 'God couldn't be anything else but a verb, a process, a relationship, with no form and no gender but animate . . .'

When Moses requested God to give him a name, as an authority to carry to Pharaoh, he asked, '"Suppose I go to the Israelites and say to them, 'The God of your fathers has sent me to you,' and they ask me, 'What is his name?' Then what shall I tell them?" God said to Moses, "I am who I am. This is what you are to say to the Israelites: I AM has sent me to you"' (Exodus 3:14–15).

If God is a verb rather than a noun, the question 'is God a what or a who?' can be answered by 'God is something to be done.' God would no longer be believed in, or confessed in faith, there would be no debate about his existence, since as God is something to be done the doing is the evidence that God is. The implication of the word 'God' being a verb is that in doing good, we 'do' God; we bring him into being. God is thus to be seen as goodness performed, just as we see the idea of dance becoming dance, and hear music only when it becomes music. God becomes because we 'do' him. Wittgenstein suggested that, 'The way you use the word "God" shows not whom you mean . . . but instead what you mean.' This can be legitimately paraphrased to read, '. . . but instead what you do'.

This discussion about the *logos* is important for understanding what is being debated, since it sets the background for the debate on key issues such a, death and survival, morality and free will, that lie behind the arguments concerning the existence of God. (See Chapter 7.)

It will be necessary to return to the subject of the language used when trying to say something about God, or to express arguments for claims that cannot be validated in the usual, empirical, way. Many philosophers have tried to use language creatively so as to give a clearer picture of what God is. Already referred to is Spinoza's, 'God as Nature', and Hegel's 'Absolute Spirit'. Closer to our time, other influential insights include A N Whitehead's 'becoming', and Paul Tillich's existentialist interpretation of 'being'.

In his 'Process Theology', Whitehead replaced the familiar ontology of 'being' with the concept of 'becoming', the 'process' referring to how concepts like purpose and meaning work themselves out sequentially as events emerging out of each other, 'like nests of Chinese boxes'. It is a holistic view of reality in which each element or 'actual entity' is part of a process of self-development; the energy or moving power in that process is God, who is also subject to change and development. This God is not the God of classical theism, omnipotent, omniscient and so on, but a God who, in Whitehead's term, 'risks' himself, by self-limitation. That is, rather than being in an over-against relationship with the world, he risks his omnipotence in what seems to be a give-and-take relationship with the world. What is important, as put by the *Stanford Encyclopaedia of Philosophy*, is that 'process theism is a genuinely *philosophical* theology in the sense that it is not grounded in claims made by special insight or revealed truths but in philosophical reflection'. The ingredients of its metaphysics are change and time, but probably because Whitehead was influenced by relativity theory and natural science, he preferred to use the phrase, 'the philosophy of organism'. This suggests that God, as process, unfolds in cycles as, for example, do plants and other organisms. In his book *Process and Reality*, Whitehead explains that, 'In all philosophical theory there is an ultimate which is capable of characterisation only through its accidental embodiments, and apart from these accidents is devoid of actuality. In the philosophy of organism this ultimate is termed "creativity"; and God is its primordial, non-temporal accident.' Whitehead is suggesting that God is a kind of model or formula of the world, or its unconscious mind; God is the power or energy behind the 'process', in which he is both changing and unchanging in the sense that while our concepts of God evolve, the essence of what is evolving is always the same. God's omnipotence or power is not used to coerce but to persuade. Whitehead's idea relies on the definition of being that Plato gives in *Sophist*: 'I hold that the definition of being is simply power.' Interestingly, Whitehead suggested that, 'In this general position the philosophy of organism seems to approximate more to some strains of Indian or Chinese thought, than to western Asiatic, or European thought. One side makes process ultimate; the other side makes fact ultimate.'

Paul Tillich's notion of the 'Ground of Being' offers a concept of God as the life-essence in which we are rooted, that essence being God's response to the threat of non-being. The concept was established in his book *The Shaking of the Foundations*, in which he explained that, 'The name of infinite and inexhaustible depth and ground of our being is God. That depth is what the word God means. And if that word has not much meaning for you, translate it, and speak of the depths of your life, of the source of your being, of your ultimate concern, of what you take seriously without any reservation. Perhaps, in order to do so, you must forget everything traditional that you have learned about God, perhaps even that word itself. For if you know that God means depth, you know much about Him. You cannot then call yourself an atheist or unbeliever. For you cannot think or say: Life has no depth! Life itself is shallow. Being itself is surface only. If you could say this in complete seriousness, you would be an atheist; but otherwise you are not.' While in a true sense, this is an existential statement its importance lies in its ontology, that is in the concept of 'being' as the basic, fundamental condition of existence. God is not an attribute of an existent object animate or inanimate, but the foundation or source from which all being emerges and in which all existent things participate. It is an interesting variation of the classical first-cause argument for the existence of God, in which God is thought to be *the* 'necessary' being. Tillich is saying that God *is* necessary being, thus freeing God from merely being a 'being'. It is a philosophical expression of the life-sustaining energy that inspired humanity's first religious responses, referred to in the previous chapter. The 'God' of Tillich is close to being a synonym for 'being-itself'.

So far the discussion has been about *what* God is, but the traditional biblical language that has conditioned our ideas about God is heavily weighted to God being a 'who', a personality with whom, as discussed in the previous chapter, it is possible to have a personal relationship. The reason for this is clear: biblical and subsequent theological language has mostly been anthropomorphic. The belief that God is a personality, with human attributes, moods and feelings, has had a very long and, for the most part, successful history, but this concept of God has become increasingly difficult to sustain. Its staying power, however, rests on more than just anthropomorphic language, since the notion of God being a person is built-in to both biblical mythology and theology. The account in Genesis tells that we were made in the image of God, 'Let us make man in our image, after our likeness' (Genesis 1:26), thus feeding our imaginations with a ready-made image of God. The concept is carried through in the theology of salvation, the messiah of Isaiah, being 'the suffering servant', a figure anticipating the role Christians understand belongs to Jesus of Nazareth as the Christ, the Son of God the Father.

The whole Bible and the Quran is full of such anthropomorphic language, and it is not difficult to understand why. Already mentioned is Moses eliciting a name from God that he could carry to Pharaoh. The 'I am who I am' referred to above can also be translated as 'I shall be that which I shall be'. It does not aid our understanding of what or who God is, beyond knowing that he is the one who is, that is the one who exists. The anthropomorphic language is therefore a kind of concession, it helps us to understand something about God by casting it in the language of human relationships. It is a way of representing what otherwise would remain abstract and abstruse. The debate about God is a debate about concepts, and for the debate to be meaningful the language in which it is conducted is critical. Atheists have criticized the language used by theists as being outmoded and we will consider the attempts made by philosophical theologians to find new, more meaningful terms.

Can the God-hypothesis be de-anthropomorphized, and what difference would it make to the debate if it was? This form of anthropomorphism is not that of children's literature, for example, giving rabbits, geese or mice, names, and allowing them to talk to each other in the reader's language; it is not the man in the moon, or Walt Disney's jungle peopled with literate animals endowed with human feelings and emotions. Even the child knows it is captive to its imagination and is able to make a distinction between these animals and its own domesticated pets.

The personifications of the Bible are far deeper, since they have become the means by which we think about the reality anthropomorphisms represent. In his article 'God and the Twenty-First Century', written for the 'spiritually progressive' Jewish magazine *Tikkun*, Michael Benedikt makes the point that, 'like metaphor in language, this form of anthropomorphism is endemic to all human perception and thought, and we just have to live with it'.

The alternative, non-anthropomorphic attempts to say something about God, referred to above, such as God is 'the ground of our being,' begin to move us in a new direction but at the price of reducing the relational quality of whatever may be experienced of the divine. Is God a Who? We have had to retain the personifications for the present. 'For the present?' – because, as already described, the God-hypothesis changes, the God of Abraham and Moses is not the same as the God of St Paul; the God of Saint Augustine is not the same as the God of Dr John A T Robinson, the controversial Bishop of Woolwich. These anthropomorphisms are born of myth and nurtured by theology. Their purpose has always been to elucidate the idea of God, to help us understand something that is probably beyond comprehension so that, at least, we may have glimpses of what it is all about. But do we need to understand? Can we not live with something as 'mystery', deriving from it the same inspiration and reassurance claimed for the conventional, received tradition of what or who God is? What is termed the '*mysterium tremendum*', that sense of inexplicable awe and mystery, has generated strong and lasting religious belief which is not dependent on anthropomorphic language, or indeed on language of any kind.

No complete picture of what God is can be given by reference only to the biblical concept. Mention has been made of religious philosophies, such as Taoism and Buddhism, that are non-theistic. Can these help us to understand what, or who, God is? To put the question differently, can Western concepts of what God is be illuminated by religious philosophies that are not dependent on a belief in God? Buddhism, for example, a religion older than those of the Bible and, like them, present throughout the world, is not centred on a belief in God, and yet it generates considerable religious energy and its followers continue to increase in number. It has been said that Buddhism hedges its bets about God, that in certain traditions of Mahayana Buddhism, clear indications of theism exist as a psychological concession to those who 'need' this kind of orientation.

One notable Zen Buddhist, the Venerable Kusala Bhikshu said, 'If you're a Buddhist it's OK to believe God was the first cause ... It really doesn't go against the teachings of the Buddha, his focus was on suffering ... It's also OK to believe science has the answer ... Like the big bang theory, etc. ... Some Buddhists don't even care how it all started, and that's fine too. Knowing how the world started is not going to end your suffering, it's just going to give you more stuff to think about ... I hope you can see that God is not what Buddhism is about.' Buddhism is about the Four Noble Truths, the fact of suffering, the causes of suffering, the cessation of suffering, and the path to liberation from it. Is it then possible, that in some traditions of Buddhism, God could be whatever it is that overcomes suffering? Might God be the energy in the realization or the enlightenment itself, that leads to nirvana? What lies at the heart of Buddhist philosophy, and what generates the energies that have sustained Buddhism for two-and-a-half-thousand years, is the process of truth displacing ignorance. To know the truth, to 'see the Light', to be enlightened, is the whole point of Buddhism, but this does not put theism at the heart of Buddhist philosophy.

The Buddhist sutras are all about 'right knowledge', that is illumination of a certain kind. Both the God-hypothesis and the Noble Path of Buddhism are concerned with the human condition, and with the nature and transformation of human consciousness. Buddhist non-theism, together with its accompanying concept of non-dualism, liberates the God-hypothesis from the idea that God might be either a 'what', or a 'who'; it broadens the ground for the debate by freeing the concept of God from the limits of the kind of language discussed above. But even a non-theistic religious philosophy with the most abstract perception of what God is, draws on metaphysics. For example, such an abstract perception of God is found in the Amitabha, 'Infinite Light' (or Pure Land), tradition of Buddhism, where the Buddha is celestial, not understood as a location but as a state of consciousness. All arguments, it seems, lead to this problem, that at the heart of the debate lies the issue of validating conceptions of God that are grounded in supernaturalism.

Chapter Three

Towards a Case for God

THE CLAIM THAT GOD EXISTS has always been strongly debated. Even among theists there has never been agreement about the nature of that God or how his existence relates to the world. The current debate has been taken up by scientists, dubbed the 'New Atheists', such as Christopher Hitchens and Richard Dawkins. In terms of logic and scientific rationalism it is not difficult to argue God out of existence, but since the methods of these disciplines are not suitable for analysing abstract concepts, this is not quite the same as actually proving God's non-existence. Nor is it possible, even with the most searching philosophical theology, to assert that God is alive and well, in such a way as to provide irrefutable proof.

Theists and atheists agree that the God-hypothesis cannot be validated by argument alone. The scientists' research into the origins of the universe led them to the theory of the 'Big Bang', including the calculation that the twenty-five elements (out of the total of ninety-two now naturally existing) necessary for anything at all to exist were present almost immediately after that enormous primordial detonation. This fact, together with the Darwinian theory of evolution, is atheism's clearest challenge to a belief in a creator-God. So far as understanding the origin of life and the physical universe is concerned, the God-hypothesis is found to be baseless and irrelevant. In response to this, theists have reformed their arguments in an attempt to show that it is 'reasonable', on other than creationist grounds, to believe God does exist. As we shall see, some of these arguments resort to logic, others to intuition, experience and history.

Whatever form the arguments take, those put forward by atheists subject the God-hypothesis to the scrutiny of natural law, to which theists respond by proposing 'laws' of a different order. Other than pantheists, those who believe God *is* everything, or panentheists, who believe he resides *in* everything, the God in which most people believe is not part of the natural order. That being so, if the existence of God is to be demonstrated, what kind of arguments can then be put forward? God is not a physical part of the universe, subject to scientific or mathematical proofs or formulas; there is no entity that we might call 'God', no specific location or observable form that we could identify as the 'Lord of the universe'. Thus, to ask if God exists is not to ask a standard scientific question.

In his *The Faith of a Physicist*, John Polkinghorne stated that, 'the question of the existence of God is the single most important question we face about the nature of reality'. Interestingly, he suggested that the quantum vacuum, a state of zero-point energy, also referred to as the cosmological constant, is the best analogy to God in the physical world. The point here is not to press the analogy, but to consider the implication that there is a need to relocate the field of the debate; that is, a discussion about the existence of God can no longer be confined to religious doctrine, theology, or philosophy, but is a subject to which modern physics must make a contribution. This broadening of the context of the debate highlights the importance not just of asking the right questions, but also of asking new kinds of questions. To put this differently, for the debate to be meaningfully engaged the issue of God's existence has to be subjected to the right kind of investigation, which may not be scientific or theological, rationalist or idealist, but an 'interdisciplinary discipline' such as Polkinghorne sees existing between, for example, chaos theory and natural theology. The discussion will return to these themes. (See Chapter 8.)

What follows is an outline of the various attempts that have been made to provide arguments for God's existence. The purpose is to introduce them here, leaving a more critical appraisal of the arguments until Chapter 4, 'The Case for Atheism'.

1. Classical Arguments for the Existence of God

The Greek philosopher Aristotle, a pupil of Plato and the teacher of Alexander the Great, has had an abiding influence on Western thought. His book *Metaphysics* is an exploration of 'being as being', from which he reasoned that God is an 'unmoved mover', and as such, an uncreated being. This is a rejection of the idea of a personal God, a creator who controls nature, in favour of an impersonal Supreme Cause. He argued that such a being was determined by a combination of what he called 'Actuality' and 'Potential'. Actuality (Gk. *energeia*) is a mode of being that can generate other beings; it is the field of events, facts and things, the 'actual' manifestation of perfection. Potentiality (Gk. *dynamis*) is not a mode in which anything exists, but represents the power for change; the ability to transform into different states is mere possibility and, as such, an imperfection. In an article for *The Catholic Encyclopaedia*, the Latin scholar Charles Herbermann explained that, for Aristotle, God was the *Actus Purus,* the absolute perfection of the absolute being. Only God can be all that could be, a fully realized potential both infinitely real and infinitely perfect. As a realized potential, God has become an actuality. The 'energy' or process that moves potentiality to actuality was thought. 'God is thinking.' In his *Metaphysics* (12.7) Aristotle wrote, 'And life also belongs to God, for the actuality of thought is life, and God is that actuality.'

In the 13th century, Thomas Aquinas developed what is probably one of the best-known contributions to the God debate. In the *Summa Theologiae*, he offered the *quinque viae*, 'Five Ways', or proofs of the existence of God. They can be simply stated:

i) The argument of the unmoved mover: Everything either moves or is moved and whatever is moved is moved by something. An endless regression is impossible, so there must exist something which moves everything else without itself being moved. This unmoved mover is God.

ii) The argument of a first cause, which is similar to the first argument in that as everything is linked in terms of cause and effect, the same endless regress is impossible thus, there must have been a first cause. This first cause is God.

iii) The argument from contingency: contingent, dependent and corruptible beings must depend on an independent and incorruptible being, the source of all necessity. This being is God.

iv) The argument from degree: the varying degrees of reality and goodness in the world must be reflections of, or approximations to, an existing absolute of these, something both perfect and unchanging. This 'something' is God.

v) The teleological argument: this is familiarly known as the argument from design in that everything in the Universe is ordered, with even lifeless things serving a purpose. This entails a Universal Orderer or designer, which is God.

Aquinas' arguments seem, in part, dependent on out-moded physics; they have been restated and reformed many times but their basic fallacies have never been successfully addressed.

Ontology, from the Greek word, *ontos* meaning, 'being' or 'that which is', is a branch of metaphysics that focuses on the nature of existence itself while making a distinction between 'real existence', and 'appearance'. One of the frequently recurring proofs for God's existence is the 'ontological argument', the most familiar form of which was first proposed by Anselm, who was Archbishop of Canterbury 1093–1109. His argument, which uses intuition and reason, begins with the notion that God is that being of which no greater can be conceived. When we hear these words, Anselm argues, we understand their meaning; in so doing we are able to accept that such a being exists even if only in terms of our thoughts. At this point the argument pauses at the question, does God exist *only* in our thoughts or does God also really exist? The argument proceeds by stating that if God existed *only* in our thoughts then it would be possible to conceive of something greater – that is, a God who exists independently of our thoughts. Hence, if God actually exists he cannot be limited to thought alone, to a mere intellectual existence but must have attributes that are greater than our mental conception of him. Anselm's argument, given in *Proslogion* II, ends confidently, 'Thus if that than which a greater cannot be conceived is in the understanding alone, then that than which a greater cannot be conceived is itself that than which a greater can be conceived. But surely this cannot be. Thus without doubt something than which a greater cannot be conceived exists, both in understanding and reality.' In a later version, Anselm offered a variation of his argument in terms of the concept of a being that cannot be conceived *not* to exist, which moves the argument from pure ontology to that of a necessary being. The logic of this latter argument is faulty and it was rejected by Aquinas, and later by various Catholic philosophers.

Kant rejected the ontological argument by denying existence as a property. He argued that if existence is part of a definition of God we are being tautological in claiming that God exists. (See the discussion on 'existence' as ascribed to God at the end of this chapter.) More positively, Kant suggests that noumena, 'things-in-themselves', are sources of experience that are not themselves knowable. Kant contrasted them with phenomena from which the noumena can be inferred. Noumena are not accessible to reason but for Kant, God can be noumenally apprehended through our moral capacity. Our knowledge of phenomena is derived from sense experience and noumena can be thought of as a sixth sense since the phenomenal is sourced in it. Other philosophers, such as Descartes and Leibniz, and, contemporarily, Alvin Plantinga and Richard Swinburne, have offered revisions of the ontological argument, each starting with a different concept of God. (See 'Further Reading'.)

2. Arguments from History

In what ways is history used as an argument for the existence of God? Believers point to biblical history, for example, as an authority for the validity of the origins of the religions it represents. That these religions have stood the test of a very long period of time is thought to vindicate what they teach and the belief invested in their teachings. In both Western and Eastern religions, tradition is of great importance, and despite the many schisms and heresies, it is the tradition that represents authority and consistency. During an interview in 1916 in the *Chicago Tribune*, Henry Ford, the founder of the Ford Motor Company, famously said, 'History is more or less bunk. It's tradition. We don't want tradition. We want to live in the present and the only history that is worth a tinker's dam is the history we made today.' Ford was reacting against a view of history as something sacrosanct, setting the precedents and traditions by which we should continue to live.

The philosophy of history distinguishes between two different ways of reading the past. A speculative philosophy of history is concerned with interpreting the past as a whole in terms of there being some form of order or design running through it, as though from a given starting point it would move towards a designated goal. In this process the philosopher of history looks for meaning and a general purposeful direction. A critical philosophy of history is concerned not with the past as such, but with the way we think about and enquire into it. It is about aims and methods, and instead of trying to discern general patterns, it breaks the field into subsidiary disciplines such as political history, social history, the history of ideas, the history of science.

For history to be used as an argument for the existence of God, the two philosophical views need to be combined. A holistic understanding of history, with its search for patterns and meaning, enables the theist to see history as a drama that plays out God's intentions for humanity. Biblical history is the paradigm for the idea that God has a plan for the world. It takes us from creation and the utopian Eden, to the 'Fall' and on through the typological history of the 'chosen people' and their promised land, to the life of Jesus of Nazareth and its salvationist purpose, thus completing the story as it began with a return of the faithful to some form of eternal paradise. The more religious history is understood as a succession of special events, the more insistent will be the claim that those events are evidence of God directing human affairs.

Such an interpretation of biblical history understands specific events to be examples of God's intervention. Examples of such events would include the Exodus, that is the liberation of the Hebrew slaves from their Egyptian captivity, together with their escape along a dry path through the Red Sea; Moses being directed to Mount Sinai to be given the Ten Commandments; God championing the Children of Israel in vanquishing their enemies so as to settle in the land gifted to them. Seen as history, the Old and New Testaments combine to tell the story of those events believed to be a demonstration of God's direct involvement in human affairs, and on the precedent of biblical history all subsequent Western history has been read in this way by followers of the biblical religions. From this point of view, all history is sacred; it is read as God's journal of his unfolding plan for the human race. (See Chapter 6 for a further discussion of the historical 'event' and its relationship to belief.)

A God of history does not have to be overtly interventionist in order to 'manage' the course of events; his influence in history can be more subtle than the great dramatic events mentioned above. Theists believe God works in cooperation with people, to form and change the nature of a developing culture by using their own creative energy and ideas and the natural human faculties of reason and imagination, by moving personal and social ethics in new directions, and by stimulating thinking minds to form new moral and political philosophies. Theists would also claim that God can inspire new theologies that challenge received traditional religious concepts and systems. Seen in this way, a God of history might well be culturally subversive, even revolutionary. In 2009, John Lennox and Christopher Hitchens debated the question 'Can Atheism Save Europe?' Lennox suggested that history demonstrates that theism in general, and Christianity in particular, inspired the scientific revolution, because it made credible that reason and intelligence are attributes of the universe. He argued that history shows Christianity to be the true foundation of European liberty, democracy and justice.

The New Testament history of the life and teachings of what Albert Schweitzer termed, the 'historical Jesus', provides its own argument for the existence of God, known as the Christological argument. The argument takes various forms, but all are based on how people understood the nature of Jesus' relationship with God. What concerns us primarily is Jesus' claim actually to *be* God. It is argued that neither he nor his disciples made such a claim and that in sayings such as John 10:30, 'I and the Father are one', the intention was to describe the intimate nature of his relationship with God rather than to assert that he and God were one and the same. To answer the Arian heresy that Jesus was only of like or similar substance to the Father, the Nicene Creed was compiled in the 4th century during the Church's first ecumenical council. It stated clearly that, Jesus is 'begotten, not made, being of *one* substance with the Father'. The doctrine that Jesus was, in fact, God is founded on an addition of lesser claims, for example that he was wise, honest, moral, not deluded, and so on, to such a degree that he was the perfect man, the 'New' or 'Second Adam', the wholly realized, actualized potential (in Aquinas' use of the terms) of what it is to be a human being. Another aspect of the Christological argument is based, not on something Jesus claimed to be, but on something that others claimed had happened to him, specifically the Resurrection. The evidence given for this lies in the New Testament accounts of the empty tomb and the post-Resurrection appearances, for example, Matthew 28, and John 20 and 21. If such an event took place, it is taken to be an act of God, hence God must exist.

The Christological argument stands or falls on whether or not Jesus was divine and, if so, in what way and to what extent, but his claim to be so is now questioned by many contemporary New Testament scholars who suggest he had divinity thrust upon him by those compiling the New Testament texts to a specific agenda. However, the God-hypothesis is not dependent on a literal belief in the Resurrection, a belief that, except within Christian fundamentalism, is losing ground.

Judaism leans heavily on a theological interpretation of history and holds it be of central importance to its faith. The record of events such as those indicated above, serves to reinforce the Jewish concept of God as a God of history. For Judaism the value of history lies in its religious and ethical content. What happened to the Jewish people from the Exodus to the foundation of the state of Israel has been interpreted and reinterpreted by Jewish religious commentators so as to cast light on 'events' as the source of religious belief and practice. The key-word for Judaism's historical argument for the existence of God is 'tradition', and how this is interpreted today has resulted in divisions between Jewish Orthodoxy and Conservative and Liberal reformers. In one sense, the survival of the Jews through history, it is claimed, offers its own proof of the existence of God: they are here now, both as a diaspora and as a nation, only because of the radical monotheism on which their faith was founded.

A spiritual encounter with God lies at the inception of Judaism and is the source of the inspiration to be found at every stage of the development of the Hebrew people and their faith. It is argued by Jewish philosophers and historians such as Maimonides and Nachman Krochmal, that Israel's religious vocation was to propagate knowledge of the Absolute Spirit, a task specifically given to it, for which it had been especially entrusted and which it has ied down the centuries. The Jewish nation and its history is thus understood to validate the existence of God.

Historical arguments for God's existence are to be found also in Islam, the tradition being that the revelation given to Muhammad from 610 CE, was written down during his lifetime to become the Qur'an. Both its historicity and its divine authorship confirm God's existence. In Islam, God is less interventionist than in the other biblical religions, but history remains the theatre in which God demonstrates his care for the world, while remaining always beyond it, or outside it. Because God intrudes less directly in human affairs, humanity has the freedom to choose its destiny, to be saved or damned. The Islamic argument from history rests on the concept of revelation.

Similar claims have been made, for example, by Joseph Smith, founder of the Mormon Church. In 1827, Smith was 'directed' by an angel called Moroni, to a place where a book of golden plates lay buried. It is these that are known as *The Book of Mormon*. The plates were inscribed with the religious history of an ancient American people, thus regaining lost truths of God's sacred history. However, such miraculous revelations and interventions seem to have declined in recent history.

The God of history, a stage director who orders events and marshals a universal cast of players to work out a drama to a given script, accords with the view that history started with a purpose and will reach an intended conclusion. This same God is also the actor who plays the principal part, and is present on the stage of history until the final curtain.

3. The Argument from Experience

Chapter 5 discusses the central and important subject of the nature of experience generally, and of religious experience in particular. Personal religious experience or, for this purpose, an experience of the biblical God, is probably the most frequently heard argument for the existence of God, and also for what is termed the 'metaphysical', a 'mode' of being which transcends physical matter and the laws of nature. Whatever kind of experience a religious experience is, it is clearly different from all other forms of experience.

If God's existence could be demonstrated by rational argument, it would dispense with the need for either experience or faith as grounds for belief. It may not be possible to know by reasoned and logical arguments, such as those offered by Aquinas, that God exists, but atheists claim that the argument for the existence of God based on experience is worthless unless it can be supported by reason. The theist's response is to argue, for example, that science and faith give access to different kinds of knowledge, on the one hand, observable, empirical knowledge that we could say is knowing *about* and, on the other hand, the kind of knowledge based on a personal and relational experience Zen Buddhists would understand as 'immediate perception'. To give a simple analogy: we can be pretty sure of the existence of His Holiness the Dalai Lama without ever having met him personally. We accept the indirect, or second-hand evidence of photographs and films, of television and radio interviews, of reading one of his books, and of the accounts and experiences of people who have been in his company. All of that provides us with one kind of knowledge of the Dalai Lama, the knowing *about* him. If we were to go to Dharamsala ourselves, and were able to spend time in the Dalai Lama's company, we would return with a direct and personal experience of having met him, and people would believe our own account because it accords with a considerable consensus of similar experience. This does not, however, seem to work with respect to God. Everyone, to some degree, knows *about* God, but not everyone is impressed by the testimony of those who claim to have 'met with' God in terms of experience. If, having experienced God ourselves, we carry that experience back to tell our friends and family about it, they are likely be sceptical. No one would be convinced of the validity of our experience of God on the strength of our account of it alone, despite the considerable consensus from others who have claimed a similar experience.

The existence of the Dalai Lama is, of course, accepted by the majority who have no first-hand experience of him. The existence of God, however, despite the testimonies of those throughout history who claim an experience of God, remains very much in doubt, and most doubters would say that only some form of clear, unambiguous, direct and personal experience, that cannot be discredited by alternative explanations, is the only thing that would convince them of God's existence. It's a case of everyone having to find out for themselves.

Under the entry on 'Empiricism' in his *A Dictionary of Philosophy*, Antony Flew explains that certainty for each of us is possible only with respect to our own experience, that an experience of God is a private and subjective matter that cannot carry to the public arena. However, almost everyone, by virtue of knowing *about* God has indirect knowledge of him; in using the word 'God' they are, at least in general terms, familiar with some of the concepts and religions hung on that word, and will make their own response to it. A claim to have experienced God is a claim to have encountered something existing independently of the one making the claim, even allowing for the criticism of hallucination and delusion and, for example, David Hume's sceptical 'perceptions of the mind'. What we cannot do, is carry into the public place the certain claim that we have experienced God, in such as way as to have it accepted as being valid. However, the argument from experience returns us to the idea that there are different kinds of knowledge each with their own principles of validation. If religious knowledge, based on experience, represents a 'special' kind of knowledge, then we have to ask if the claim to a special kind of experience is evidence of God's existence.

In *The Will to Believe*, a lecture published in 1896, the psychologist William James defended religious faith even though there was no objective evidence of the claims made by that faith. Scientists set out to inquire into something simply on the strength of a hypothesis; they begin by looking for evidence that will advance their research. They research to find out *if* something is true. It can be argued that a life of faith is research of another kind, a way of living so as to discover *if* God exists. It was exactly this approach, recorded in the *Kalama Sutra*, that the Buddha recommended, 'Do not accept any of my words on faith, believing them just because I said them . . . Only accept what passes the test by proving useful and beneficial in your life.'

Much religion is cast in the tension of the father's plaintive plea to Jesus, 'I believe; help my unbelief!' (Mark 9:24). There is always uncertainty in the process of trying to validate any hypothesis, since all research is speculative until adequate data is able either to prove or disprove it. Something can be discovered to be true simply by taking the Buddha's advice and living as though the proposition was true. In that process, if it is found to be 'true for you', then the invested belief or faith may become knowledge. (The relationships between faith, reason and knowledge are discussed in Chapter 6.)

In the essay referred to above, James also argues that accepting evidence for the truth of something believed can itself be dependant on belief, he says, 'The desire for a certain kind of truth here brings about that special truth's

existence; and so it is in innumerable cases of other sorts.'
It seems that James is getting close to saying that religious
truth based on faith is self-authenticating, even wish-
fulfilling; if so, it is not going to help verify the argument
from experience. The problem is that in matters of belief,
whether based on experiences of love, morality or aesthetics,
a belief cannot be demonstrated to be true, even though
that belief may be derived from experience of something
in the phenomenal world, such as something terrifying or
beautiful. What James leaves us with is 'the right to believe',
and 'the need to believe'. In terms of psychology, belief
is rational even though there is no evidence for it. These
ideas will recur in Chapter 5, when the particular nature of
religious experience is considered. For the present, James
postulates two forms of the argument from experience.
The strong form states simply that religious experience can
be evidence of the existence of God or other supernatural
phenomenon, for anyone. The weak form of the argument
suggests that religious experience is evidence only for the
person claiming it.

Religious experience is only one of many kinds of
what can be termed abstract experience, others being, for
example, ethical or aesthetic. For empiricist philosophers
our experience is the accumulated data we receive of the
world through the senses. For rationalist philosophers like
Kant, experience is not passively received by a mind that
is blank, a *tabula rasa*. Kant argues that all our experience
is processed by means of constant reflection given by the
individual to his myriad encounters with the world and
with other people. Among these experiences will be those
understood to be religious, but if so, even though they are
first received by the senses, for example from listening to
music, that sense experience will be transcended. We will
need to consider more fully what William James termed,
'the varieties of religious experience', and in so doing

return to the question as to whether or not such experience constitutes evidence for the existence of God.

4. The Concept of God in non-Western Religions

It has already been noted that, in general, the Eastern perception of God is markedly different to that of the biblical religions which have taken the brunt of the atheists' criticisms. The leading New Atheists have given little consideration to the claims of Eastern religious traditions and without doing so their case must remain incomplete. Buddhism, in particular, is non-theistic, and behind the polytheism of Hinduism, lies a monism, a belief in some ultimately unifying principle, rather than in a personal God. The many gods of the various Hindu traditions are not an end in themselves, but a means of finally transcending the kaleidoscopic world of appearance so as to perceive and be absorbed in Brahman. Brahman is conceived as eternal, infinite and unchanging, both immanent and transcendent.

The 8th-century Hindu philosopher, Adi Shankara developed a non-dualistic concept of the soul's unity with Brahman. He stated that, 'Brahman is the only truth, the spatio-temporal world is an illusion, and there is ultimately no difference between Brahman and the individual self.' However, Shankara also said that logic alone cannot establish the existence of this unity as ultimate reality. His system is built around a combination of reason and experience, but reason can only take you so far. Experiencing the existence of Brahman is the only way of knowing the Ultimate exists. While he taught his students the importance of being grounded in Vedic tradition, he gave equal importance to their personal experience. However difficult it is to verify or to describe its nature, an experience of Brahman is founded on logic, grammar and linguistic analysis (*vyakarana*) and on *mimamsa*, the art of interpretation that enables the student to elucidate the Vedic texts. These logical and intellectual disciplines are the basis for the kind of experience that leads to the unity of the *atman* (self) with the ultimate principle, Brahman. The Hindu god Krishna, understood as 'eternal existence', has similar attributes to the monotheistic God of the Bible and, as with that God, his existence cannot be proved rationally.

However, Hinduism does offer one argument for the existence of God and that is karma, something regarded as an aspect of natural law. Karma is a vast subject, and we cannot dwell on it other than to say it is a law of cause and effect; there is a link between action, intention, thoughts and their consequences. Everything we do or think has a knock-on effect accumulated as good or bad karma, the balance of which will determine the nature (quality) of our rebirth. Shankara argued that karma presumed the existence of a supreme being whose power or energy ensures that what we sow we reap. The Nyaya school, Hinduism's school of logic, also offered the doctrine of karma as proof of the existence of God. Since the consequences of a person's actions may not work themselves out until the next life, there must be some kind of agency that carries such things forward through a person's reincarnation. That agency is thought of, by some, as God.

Although the Buddha did not encourage a belief in God, a similar argument, based on karma, is to be found in Buddhism. For Buddhists, what directs karma is more easily identified as an ethical system, based on the Eightfold Path, and the extent to which this is honoured determines the karmic future of the individual. Behind this, for example, lies the idea that the concept of goodness, in relative terms, can only have meaning if goodness takes an absolute form. Only because the practitioner knows that there is a 'greatest good', can sense be made of any effort to be a good person. Richard Hayes, a professor of Buddhist philosophy at the

University of New Mexico, has explained that the attitude of the Buddha to God was not atheistic, but anti-speculative: there is no point in using time and energy in arguing about something that can never be proved. Professor Hayes wrote, 'the Buddha Gautama is portrayed not as an atheist who claims to be able to prove God's non-existence, but rather as a sceptic with respect to other teachers' claims to be able to lead their disciples to the highest good' (*Journal of Indian Philosophy,* January 1988).

5. Arguments against Atheism

The atheists' claim that there is no rational or valid reason to believe in the existence of God leaves them with the same dilemma as for believers: how we can know that what we know is true? To put this another way, how can we validate the claim that experience, or even the lack of it, is its own authority? To respond to this question fully, atheists would need to give some consideration to different modes of reality. Generally, they are reluctant to allow even the possibility of there being different kinds, or degrees of reality, such as an empirical and verifiable reality, or a reality 'of another order', which is convincing to those who claim to perceive it but who cannot demonstrate its validity by the usual means. The need to be sure about the reality of certain kinds of phenomena has led to a wide variety of experiment and research in pursuit of, for example, ghosts and poltergeists, of UFOs and spirit possession, of the validity of so-called faith-healings, all of which break the restraints of natural law. What is surprising is that atheists who eschew metaphysics on scientific grounds are prepared to research the claims of, for example, telepathy and pyschokinesis (or telekinesis), even though these phenomena are thought to contravene the laws of physics. Claims for the existence of God have been around for so long, and take so many different forms, that it seems inadequate for atheists to dismiss these merely because they also don't conform to physical law, logic and reason.

The following is a brief excursion into theism's arguments against atheism.

i)   Atheism can only exist in relation to a concept of God. But there are so many different and opposed concepts of God, that atheists need to face the question as to what God, or what kind of God is being denied. Usually an atheist is someone who denies all forms of God but, as we shall see in the following chapter, there are different forms of atheism. Even in a religious context, anyone believing in their own perception of God (for example Baruch Spinoza), who denies the validity of alternative views of God, stands as an atheist in relation to those believers. Thus, depending on one's point of view, atheism can be understood as a form of heresy. In his influential book *The God Delusion*, Richard Dawkins declares that his main interest is Christianity and that he won't be paying any particular attention to other religions such as Buddhism or Confucianism. His point, presumably, is that demolishing one concept of God, demolishes them all.

ii)   Atheists should be asked to prove God's non-existence. Why should atheists assume that the onus of proof is on the believer? In a sense, disproving God's existence is what modern atheism is aiming to do by subjecting the God-hypothesis to the scrutiny of the laws of physics, but as the God adhered to is, by definition, inscrutable to such laws, atheism is unable to demonstrate God's non-existence. Atheists can only conclude that God does not exist on the criteria of their own arguments.

iii) Atheists fail to take into account the use and nature of language. To talk about God is not the same as talking about another person, an animal, a place or a thing. It is as difficult to use words to establish the existence of God, as it is to convince a person born blind, of the existence of light. Because God's existence cannot be demonstrated in terms of sense experience, atheists might be better giving thought to the different kinds of experience on which belief is based and the language used to express it.

iv) It is argued that the New Atheism fails to respond to our basic human needs. In his book *What's So Great About Christianity?* Dinesh D'Sousa wrote, 'atheism fails to answer any of man's most important questions or satisfy his deepest needs'. Some of our deepest needs are expressed by questions such as 'Where have I come from?' and 'Why am I here?' The scientific answers to these questions fall short of what is termed 'the anthropic principle', an important philosophical method of enquiry introduced in 1973 by the theoretical physicist Brandon Carter. He explains that the anthropic principle is one of balance between the way we observe the world and the way we are conscious of it, that our observation of the physical world must be compatible with the human consciousness that observes it. For some, consciousness will disclose the existence of God because of a disposition to do so, while for others, differently disposed or orientated, God's existence will not be discerned. Radical atheism does not allow for the validity of one or other of these possibilities. In fact, atheism dismisses the first possibility as an incompatibility between the observer and his consciousness of the physical world. However, this argument against atheism only leads to a kind of 'live and let live', an uneasy co-existence of our contradictory observations of the physical universe.

v) In making the assertion that God's existence cannot be proved, atheists do not give proper consideration to the function of faith. The epistemological theory of

fideism (Latin *fides,* faith, thus faith-ism) states that faith
is independent of reason, being concerned with truths to
which reason has no access. Kierkegaard, dubbed 'the father
of Existentialism', represented an extreme form if fideism
by stating that religion requires us to accept concepts that
are actually absurd, totally contrary to reason. In contrast,
for example, St Augustine of Hippo or Pascal represented
a less extreme form of fideism by suggesting that, while
incompatible, faith and reason can work together, reason
playing a secondary role in enabling some understanding
of what can only be known by faith. It is a compromise
atheism disallows, even though the scientific process of
research and experiment proceeds by precisely this kind of
balanced cooperation between reason and faith.

vi)   Atheism does not offer a persuasive account of the
origins of morality, or of our aesthetic sense and perceptions. Our moral sense, they argue is not God-given but
is a inborn function built into a group's social ethics on the
secular principle of 'do unto others as you would be done
by'. Aesthetics, our sense of beauty and proportion, is
similarly innate and a specific expression of what we hold,
generally, to be 'good'. Thrown back on secular humanism,
it is argued that atheists can only settle for relative standards
of human behaviour which, nevertheless, they measure by
standards of ultimate goodness and justice. Theists contend
that any alternative to these ultimate forms derived from
an ultimate being, leads to a do-it-yourself morality which
is, at best, subjective, self-interested and anarchic. God, it
is argued, provides the benchmark for moral and aesthetic
standards.

vii)   Theists argue that atheism is not equipped to judge
assertions about God, since it has no understanding of
theology. Scientists who are also theists, such as Professor
John Polkinghorne, have a far better grasp of science than

atheists have of theology. Terry Eagleton, in *Reason, Faith, and Revolution: Reflections on the God Debate*, makes this point, 'An atheist who has more than a primitive (one might say Satanic) understanding of theology is as rare as an American who has been abducted by aliens.' The argument here is that atheists are incompetent, that they have failed to understand the claims of theists, and that they have challenged these claims entirely on their own terms. It is a charge that picks up on themes already covered, that atheists and theists stand on different ground, make claims of a different order, and use validation criteria within the terms of reference of their own discipline.

In closing this chapter on the case for God, an important point has to be added. It concerns the use of the word 'existence', when attributed to God. Arguing for, or against, the existence of God raises the issue of the meaning of existence itself. The argument has been waged all down the years between theists and atheists, and between philosophers and theologians, without sufficient consideration being given to what it means to claim that God 'exists'. Paul Tillich argued, in his *Systematic Theology*, Part 1, that it is wrong to speak of God as 'existing', because to do so reduces God to 'finite potentialities' and such a God, could not be, what Tillich termed, 'the ground of our being'. To say that God exists, reduces God to the status of a mere entity among other beings, in other words, the attribute 'existence', is a form of anthropomorphism that ascribes to God the kind of 'beingness' everything has, so as to be able to understand God's existence in terms of our own. The result is that the concept of God is hypostatized, that is construed as 'real'. This is expressed, for example, in the Christian doctrine of incarnation. Christianity might be able to speak of the existence God in the form of Jesus, since in that *form* God can be held to have existed. In using the word, 'existence', earlier philosophers and theologians had in mind an 'idea' of God as truth, as a reality, but as such the concept of God resided only in people's minds and not as an existence per se. Only a God that exists as an absolute being can be of service to human beings who are conscious of their limitation in time and space, and who live with the knowledge of their mortality. Atheists tend to miss this point entirely, and the foregoing discussion serves to heighten the problem of arguing from different premises, and of using language that serves neither cause.

If the existence of God could be proved, whatever that proof disclosed would not be God, it would be just another 'thing' that existed. What all forms of God represent, from the Brahma of the Hindu Vedanta to the incarnate God of the New Testament, is 'ultimate reality', that is, *the* ultimate reality, not *an* ultimate reality, since the ultimate can be only be one, or One. If this ultimate reality were to turn out to be an m-string theory or formula, or a series of them, the question becomes, not does God exist, but is it necessary to ascribe divinity to the m-string theory in order to appreciate and understand its special significance? Since such a theory is part of the natural, physical world, we can dispense with the quality 'supernatural', and since we are dealing with the physical, we are no longer involved with the misty realm of the metaphysical, and are close to associating God with the much sought-after 'theory of everything'. The implications of this are developed in Chapter 8.

Chapter Four

The Case for Atheism

IF PROOF FOR THE EXISTENCE OF GOD is dependent on the kind of evidence required by scientists, then it would seem the atheists have won the debate. What they require is clear and unequivocal:

i) That any claim for God's existence should be demonstrated in the same way as is the existence of anything, that is empirically, by reference to natural law.

ii) That similar proof be given for the dimension or 'realm' termed 'metaphysical', which, even if God does not exist, is claimed as a source of spiritual experience.

Generally, an atheist is thought of as someone who denies the existence of God, and in a culture conditioned more by religion than any other influence, it is not surprising that throughout most of its history the word 'atheist' has been used pejoratively. As we have seen, there are movements within some religions that are non-theistic, owing nothing to biblical concepts of God. For example, Hinduism's ancient Vedic perception, particularly its oldest philosophical school, Sankhya, teaches there are as many souls and units of consciousness as that there are living beings. This view is distinctive in understanding that all these souls, indeed all individual consciousness, is to be absorbed in the eternal, absolute being, Brahman.

Carvaka, another school of philosophical Hinduism, tends towards materialism and non-theism, as do Jainism and some major traditions of Buddhism.

Atheism has been around for a long time. In ancient Greece the term *atheos* meant 'without god'. It was then used polemically, as the word 'heathen' is used today, to label those who deny one's own conception of the divine. Even though Jews and Christians believed in their own God, they were accused by the Romans of atheism because they refused to acknowledge the gods of Rome, and specifically the divinity of the emperor. The word moved on to be used by Christians against heretics, even those who, while believing in God, denied the Trinity. Spinoza earned the reputation of being an atheist, because he failed to make a clear distinction between a concept of God and the natural world, and was, at best, accused of pantheism. Atheism, became more narrowly defined with the development of i) secularism and attendant concepts such as materialism, which in philosophy holds that only matter exists and that everything is entirely dependent on it, and ii) humanism, a rational system of thought which gives centre place to human beings, rather than to divine or supernatural beings.

Humanism, in its various forms, advanced the cause of atheism. Alexander Pope's *Essay on Man* is close to being a humanist manifesto. The term 'Humanism', familiar as the characteristic theme of Renaissance Europe, exemplified during the 18th-century Enlightenment a broad love of humanity. It was a world-view which rejected all religion on the grounds that to be actively concerned with human well-being called for reliance on human resources alone. Prime movers in the Enlightenment included the political theorists and philosophers Edmund Burke and Jean-Jacques Rousseau.

Later, in the 19th century the humanist cause was taken up by a group of philosophers referred to as the Young or Left Hegelians. Particularly influential was Ludwig Feuerbach, who claimed that God had been invented, and that all religious beliefs and practices were expressions of wish-fulfilment. This was an assertion that influenced, for example, Karl Marx and Friedrich Nietzsche, the latter famous for his 'God is dead' thesis. In the 20th century, the case for atheism was taken up by philosophers of language, such as Wittgenstein, Russell and Ayer, whose purpose was to apply a rigorous rationalism to language in general, and to the language used to express metaphysical concepts in particular. Atheism's influence on political philosophy led to the establishment of secular states in which religion was suppressed, as happened in Stalin's Soviet Union, and other communist countries that imposed what can be termed a state atheism. Mikhail Bakunin, the Russian theorist of collectivist anarchism, paraphrased Voltaire's 'If God didn't exist it would be necessary to invent him', as 'If God really existed, it would be necessary to abolish him.' He also argued that to believe God exists is the negation of human liberty and requires an abdication of reason and justice that results in 'the enslavement of mankind, in theory and practice'.

Broadly speaking atheism, as the absence of belief, is found in various forms. Strong and weak atheism, known also as positive or negative atheism, represent the views of the majority of non-believers. Strong, or positive atheism stands on the claim that God does not exist, holding that such an assertion is logically impossible. It denies the existence of any kind of divinity whether polytheistic or monotheistic. Weak, or negative atheism, states that there is no verifiable evidence or good reason to suppose that God does exist; this form of atheism includes agnosticism, the view that regardless of what atheists or theists assume, it is impossible actually to know whether or not God exists. Some philosophers, such as the logical positivists Russell and Ayer, argue that because the claim 'God exists' is meaningless, it falls outside the field of reasonable inquiry and is thus, neither true nor false. Veracity can only be accorded to something that has meaning.

To these various forms of atheism, implicit, explicit, positive, negative, theoretical, or practical, can be added, metaphysical atheism. This is an implicit denial of God in all the forms in which the concept normally appears in both philosophy and theology, while accepting the existence of an Absolute, but one that does not possesses any of the attributes traditionally accorded to God, such as transcendence, personal character, omniscience, and so on. While for the debate atheists focus on the biblical concept of God, the argument is that the God-hypothesis is not necessarily confined to the concept of a single divine entity of the kind presented in the Bible, since there is a non-theistic alternative that accounts for the 'oneness', or homogeneity of reality. The appeal is to a form of monism, the view that there is an inherent unity described, for example, by the concepts of pantheism or panentheism, an indwelling entity that is simply 'there', but not made known by revelation, or subject to the doctrines and theologies of religion. What is rejected is the creator God of the Bible; what stands in place of it is a principle, or energy, that accounts for the homogeneity of reality. If this is fully understood we would, as Hawking put it, know the mind of God. In proposing a unifying being, energy or principle, the concept of metaphysical atheism is a radical compromise of other forms of atheism, but it is gathering momentum in the God-debate as a bridge-builder between what otherwise are irreconcilable positions.

In the brave new world of the New Atheists there are no compromises at all; atheists stand on the positive affirmation, 'I don't believe in the existence of any sort of God, spirit, or metaphysical life force.' From this unequivocal statement the case for atheism broadens out to a wide range of arguments, the principal themes of which are: Creation; Creationism and Evolution; and the Problem of Evil and Suffering.

1. Creation

The problem of origins provides atheists with clear reasons for questioning the God-hypothesis. The rejection of the biblical creation account as myth was brought about by the 'progressive revelation' of science, a process which began with the scientific revolution in the 17th century. It is not possible to reconcile a literal belief in the accounts of God's creation of the universe in six days, with the theory of a Big Bang that occurred some thirteen and a half billion years ago; nor does the idea that we are made in the image of God lie comfortably with the Darwinian theory that human beings owe their origin to a subhuman species. Interestingly, the kinds of questions with which the Genesis accounts were concerned still resonate with people, both scientists and theists, believers and non-believers, who continue to ask 'Where do I come from?' or 'Why am I here?' The writers of Genesis would certainly have had questions such as these in mind, but they were not the reason why the accounts were compiled. The Hebrew stories were fed by Babylonian legends, themselves built into the earliest history of Mesopotamia, and carried to Palestine by the legendary figure of Abraham.

The Christian and Islamic adoption of the same stories seems unlikely as one might have thought that the world had moved on by the time of the inter-testamental period, that is from the time of the writing of Malachi (*c.* 420 BCE), the last of the Old Testament prophets, to the appearance of John the Baptist in the 1st century CE, and certainly by the time of Muhammad. It is surprising there were no new accounts of the origins of life and the universe more suitable to their own times, philosophies and perceptions. As noted in Chapter 1, the writer of John's Gospel made a strong attempt to do this when he moved the narrative from myth to philosophical theology by introducing the *logos* doctrine, 'In the beginning was the Word . . .' At least, in this respect, the concept was in tune with 1st-century patterns of thought.

This invites the question of what kind of modern myths might be drafted today that would prove relevant to the conflicting ideas of this debate? This question will be answered in several ways in later chapters, but the weaving of modern myths may be found in science-fiction films like *Matrix*, and in the books of, for example, Tolkien, William Golding and Philip Pullman that continue to explore the basic questions and to search for answers to the perennial problems of good and evil, the breakdown of civil order, and the notion that chaos lies just below the surface of our civilization.

The two basic questions about the origin and purpose of human life – Where do I come from? Why am I here? – have not only been asked by the Babylonian-Hebraic myth-makers, but have been posed by all cultures, regardless of the character of their religions. For example, the Kalahari Bushmen tell stories about the making of their world and the universe by proto-ancestors; the Australian aboriginals are custodians of an oral tradition that talks of powerful ancestors deep in their history, stories that sound like recovered memories of an ancient past. The Maya tell of their origin from corn, the raw material from which human beings were made; the Norse myths speak of Odin and Ymir; the *Kojiki*, the Japanese, *Record of Ancient Things*, compiled between 500 and 700 CE, contains accounts of Izanagi 'the male who invites', and Izanami 'the female who invites'; the Brihad-arayaka Upanishad, written

600–700 BCE, recounts that recounts that 'In the beginning, this universe was the self [Viraj] alone, in the shape of a person.' The 'self' is the energy for creation and everything that exists does so as a result of the self reflecting on itself. Such questions are clearly of universal interest. Atheists argue that the theory of evolution, and the discoveries of astrophysicists about the Big Bang origin of the universe, render the God-hypothesis irrelevant since they provide rational accounts both of our origins and the purpose of life. But, to understand what is being debated, concepts of creation and of our origins need more discussion.

At the heart of the creation debate is the problematic idea of creating something out of nothing. If, in the beginning, there was *only* God, how was creation started and with what substances? Augustine of Hippo made a thoughtful contribution to the discussion in recognizing the difficulty of interpreting the creation stories literally. He offered a surprising answer to the question, saying that what God created with was time. If, '"In the beginning God made heaven and earth." It must be inferred that God had created nothing before that; "in the beginning" must refer to whatever he made before all his other works. Thus, there can be no doubt that the world was not created "in" time but with time' (*Confessions* XI, Ch. 6). The controversial ecumenical theologian Hans Küng suggested Augustine's assertion that God created *with* time was one that Einstein might have understood. Augustine again: 'It is in eternity, which is supreme over time because it is a never-ending present, that you are at once before all past time and after all future time' (*Confessions* XI, Ch. 13). The theistic doctrine of eternity is not to be confused with never-ending time, it lies before time. In the March 2010 edition of the journal *Tikkun*, Küng comments, 'thus, from a theological perspective the act of creation is a timeless act; it comes about through time. And time is created time, created time-space, created space-time.' Cosmologists also suggest that time was created with the Big Bang, and they too must wrestle with the question as to what existed before this event.

Somewhat like the Buddhists, the cosmologists seem unconcerned to account for what existed originally, that is before the Big Bang and the creation of time. Is it possible that with the concept of time as the 'medium' of creation, the debate might touch on common ground? Or if not on the subject of time, then on the idea of creation out of nothing? Both parties are faced with the same proposition that if, originally, there was nothing, how do we conceive of that 'nothing', was it just space, or a limitless black hole? Both of these are something. If the nothing was absolute then it excludes the possibility that creation was kicked off by anything material. Theists, however, hold to the notion that God is eternal, even when there was nothing, a notion hard to reconcile since the concept 'eternal' can only be understood over against the qualifying concept of a limiting factor in time. God cannot exist as anything that 'came into being', since that implies there was a time when he 'was not'. Nor can it be claimed that God exists 'by and from the self' as an act of self-creation, as suggested by the Upanishad referred to earlier, since if God is eternal, he is uncreated.

The debate about creation thus sets up the conflict between the theological *creatio ex nihilo*, creation out of nothing, and the physicists' *creatio ex materia*, creation out of some form of ever-existing matter, although the jury is still out about what actually existed before the Big Bang. Standard models of the universe suggests that both time and space began with the Big Bang some 13 million years ago. Together with the theory of a singularity that existed at the time of the Big Bang are theories of multiple universes co-existing side by side, as the Astronomer Royal, Martin

Rees put it, 'like bubbles of foam'. The Demiurge of Plato's *Timaeus* is described as shaping already existing material, and represents an 'energy' that is not the creator, whereas the God of Genesis, in as much as the creation seems to emerge out of nothing, is both creator and sustainer of what is created. If such a creator were to withdraw his support then, as Archbishop William Temple put it, the universe would 'collapse into non-existence'.

The cosmologists of the new astrophysics, even allowing for the unimaginable time sequences involved in the process of putting the universe together, are not eternalists and they tell us life on Earth will last only as long as the Sun supports it. Beyond that, rival scientific theories suggest that, as each of the uncountable numbers of stars in each of the innumerable universes dies, the universe itself may cease to exist, or revert to a singularity, or freeze up, or that it will be torn apart by what is nicknamed 'the Big Rip'. Against such theories atheism's disbelief in the creator God of the Bible seems unassailable. However, those who believe in the biblical God do not seriously consider that God will withdraw his support, and simply stand by while the solar system implodes, rather do they hold to that theory of history in which everything is moving, in evolutionary mode, towards some form of perfection, and that the Earth will, somehow, be restored to its Edenic model of paradise.

Whether or not God exists, for physicists 'nothingness' cannot exist for, as the phrase has it, 'nature abhors a vacuum'. However, the idea of anything being literally empty may be tenable, since 'nothingness' can be understood as a quantum vacuum, a state in which quantum fields, with matter such as photons, electrons, quarks and so on, do not exist. Even so, Professor John Polkinghorne assures us that, 'it does not mean that nothing is going on. Quite the contrary, for the vacuum in quantum theory is a humming hive of activity.' It seems, then, that for science the notion of creation out of nothing is a non-starter, and that the atheists have won the creationist part of the argument.

2. Creationism and Evolution

The case for atheism holds that the Big Bang theory is an alternative offered by science to the Genesis account of the origin of the universe. Furthermore, atheists consider that such disciplines as palaeontology and evolutionary biology provide rational explanations of the origin and development of the life this planet supports. There is no need here to explain the principles of the theory of evolution since, in general terms, the concept is understood; but because it holds a central place in the case for atheism it will be necessary to keep referring to it, since theists have made a positive response to its challenge. Atheists contend that to argue against evolution is to argue for the floating zoo that was Noah's ark but, in general, they fail to take sufficient account of the fact that this form of creationism is held only by biblical fundamentalists, and that theists have responded with a new, 'progressive', demythologized theology that sees the hand of God in the evolutionary process.

Scholars such as Rabbi Arthur Green and Professor Hans Küng suggest that evolution, far from undermining the Genesis account of the activities of a creator God, tells us *how* God created. Professor Küng writes in *Tikkun*, 'The human being, not isolated, but in the midst of the cosmos, is the great goal of the process of creation.' Rabbi Green, in the same edition of *Tikkun*, proposed that evolution, 'is a place, even *the* place, where the sacred waits to be discovered. There is a One that reveals itself to us within and behind the great diversity of life. That One is Being itself, the constant in the endlessly changing evolutionary parade.' This is a mind-set that, having abandoned biblical literalism and timescales, endeavours to hold to both God and the Big Bang, and, grateful to the 'revelation' of science, regards evolution as a description of how God went about his work. The thought is that evolution may be one of the many tools used by God in the creative process. Karl E Peters, co-editor of *Zygon: Journal of Religion and Science*, attempts to reconcile the opposed views by suggesting a concept of God that rests on Darwinian ideas of random variation and natural selection. The argument is that God is not the Creator, but the creative process of which evolution is a part. Peters writes, 'by participating in the creative process we are dancing with the sacred'. Here, Peters is offering a modern form of the process theology referred to in the previous chapter.

It is doubtful that atheists would be impressed by any of these attempts at theological–biological syncretisms, since they remain based in metaphysics. However, such attempts as Peters's at a reconciliation of evolution and creationism illustrate what is referred to as 'spiritual evolution', a concept that has a broad agenda ranging from cosmology to personal experience. It links with an issue not considered by opponents of the God-hypothesis, that is an alternative concept of time being cyclic rather than linear. Such a view is held, for example, by the Maya, Hinduism, Kabbalism, the Indian pacifist religion Jainism, and by Buddhism, and it has also found it way into Western literature and poetry. In these religious and philosophical systems, evolution is carried through immense cycles of time, and concerns not just the physical world but the gradual unfolding of human spirituality. Spiritual evolution, whether based on the God-hypothesis or not, is seen to be so fundamental to the survival of our race that it could have been naturally selected, as if etched on our genes to form part of our DNA.

The emanationist view of spiritual evolution, character-istic, for example, of Sufism, Hindu Sankhya philosophy and the Eastern Orthodox Church, understands creation as a series of hierarchically descending radiations from the Godhead which, through intermediate stages, leads to its expression in matter. Leaving the Godhead aside, this emanationist view might easily fit the modern atheist-cosmologists' account of the evolution of everything from the moment of the Big Bang. Despite these alternative syncretistic readings of evolution, the case for atheism seems to remain intact since the source of the hierarchical radiations, the Godhead, remains open to the same demands of validity as as are required to demonstrate the existence of the biblical God.

Atheists have been faced with many other demyth-ologizing attempts to bring about some form of coexistence between creation and evolution and, more broadly, science and religion, a cause to which Einstein made his famous contribution, 'Science without religion is lame; religion without science is blind.' But even though Einstein seemed to hold to the idea of some form of intelligence under-pinning the universe, atheists are unlikely to concede that science is handicapped by the lack of religion.

The attempt to combine a philosophical and religious description of reality with that of science has a distinguished history. It has given us Henri Bergson, who took the view that intuition and immediate experience give a more valid perception of reality that rationalism or science. What he termed the *Élan Vital* is a vital impetus or creative urge that displaces natural selection at the heart of evolution. His philosophy combines the creative impulse responsible for the universe with the creative impulse within every human being. A N Whitehead's concept of 'process philosophy' was mentioned above and in Chapter 2. It understands evolution to be a process by which God offers possibilities which may, or may not, be realized; the 'process' is seen as inherently creative, understanding evolution as a model of how change and innovation operate in nature. It is both destabilizing and the cutting-edge of variation and novelty, and one in which God evolves along with everything else. Teilhard de Chardin also understood evolution as an uncertain process that 'offers' potentials that include what he termed 'cosmogenesis'. For Teilhard it all began with the formation of atoms, molecules and inanimate matter, continuing with the biosphere and organic evolution, then with man and the world of human thought, for which he coined the term 'noosphere'. Everything continues on to the end of being unified in the Omega Point, which for Teilhard was Jesus Christ. Evolution is thus the basic mode of necessary and inevitable change which moves everything along from origin to perfection.

Dr Joel Primack is a physicist who specializes in the theory of cold, dark matter. Somewhere, within this specialization, he finds space to believe in God. In *Scientists Comment on Faith*, he writes, 'In the last few years astronomy has come together so that we are now able to tell a coherent story [of how the universe began.] This story does not contradict God, but instead enlarges [the idea of] God.'

As thorough-going and appealing as some of these theological modifications of evolution might be, they are unlikely to make any impression with the 'strong' atheists and again we are brought back to the recurring problem that none of them offers a sound empirical basis, or any acceptable means of verification.

The process of evolution has given atheists a form of secular religion referred to as evolutionary humanism, a world-view that abandons the God-hypothesis as wholly unnecessary not only to our understanding of origins but also as a basis for morality and aesthetics. The phrase, 'evolutionary humanism' is associated with the biologist Julian Huxley, who was a major player in putting together the mechanistic form of the theory of evolution known as 'the evolutionary synthesis'. His concept of humanism includes the proposition that, if evolution is the fundamental process of all universal change, then whatever it is that causes or blocks change can be thought of as being respectively, 'good' or 'bad'. For evolutionary humanists, the moral sense is itself a product of evolutionary change, rather than something inherent or derived from a supernatural source. Yet Huxley made no disavowal of the God-hypothesis, just a plea that it should be recast in new terms. In *Essays of a Humanist*, Huxley wrote, 'There is no separate supernatural realm: all phenomena are part of one natural process of evolution. There is no basic cleavage between science and religion. I believe a drastic reorganization of our pattern of religious thought is now becoming necessary, from a god-centred to an evolutionary-centred pattern.' This, again, seems to take the case for a compromise between theists and non-theists back to an emanationist view of creation and a kind of pantheism or panentheism

It has to be said that 'strong' atheism cannot accommodate any form of compromise, let alone a syncretism that aims to form an alliance between science and religion, unless valid proof can be given. The question remains as to whether the criteria on which such judgements about validity are made are themselves valid, a question that will be considered in Chapter 7.

3. The Problem of Evil and Suffering

For theists this has always been the most intractable of all problems, for atheists a seemingly unanswerable argument against the existence of God. Theists resort to a theodicy, a theology that aims to vindicate the goodness and justice of an all-loving God who 'allows' evil to function in the world he created. The term 'theodicy' was coined by the German philosopher Gottfried Leibniz in his *Theodicy Essays on the Goodness of God, the Freedom of Man and the Origin of Evil,* and it will be considered later in the discussion.

A necessary distinction needs to be made between 'evil' and 'suffering'. In Western culture evil forms part of the deeply entrenched dualism represented by God and the Devil, and the familiar derivative pairs, good and evil, saint and sinner, and so on. The manifestations and consequences of evil carry the moral connotations of something that is wrong, blameworthy, or reprehensible. But usually the term 'evil' is specifically associated with the malignant force or power emanating from the Devil or Satan, to which the power of God is opposed. In short, Western dualism regards human life as a stage on which the conflict between good and evil is fought out. The distinction to be born in mind is that evil always causes suffering, but not all suffering stems from evil. An individual, or regime, can be said to be evil, or driven by an evil power if it is responsible for deliberately causing suffering to others, as has happened all through history. But the sufferings caused by disease, anxiety, natural disaster, or the misunderstandings that constantly occur between people, are not thought of as evil, since they have a natural cause. However, there are theists who, holding to the Genesis story of Eden, understand that the whole of creation was cursed in the moment of Eve's disobedience to God, believing that even the powers and processes of nature are, by consequence, evil. In Jewish theology that proto-disobedience was the outward sign of God having been forsaken, and it is this separation from God that is believed to be the source of all the 'curses, confusion, frustration, in all that you undertake to do, until you are destroyed and perish quickly, on account of the evil of your doings, because you have forsaken me' (Dueteronomy

28:20). The Old Testament doctrine of 'the Fall' is carried through into the New Testament in the concept of 'original sin', and on throughout history by successive generations of theologians such as Aquinas, Luther and Calvin. For atheists, earthquakes and floods, hurricanes and volcanoes, famines, epidemics and all forms of disease, however extreme the resultant suffering may be, are not thought of as evil, but simply as morally neutral powers of nature.

Atheists argue that the entire issue of evil and suffering, however the causes of these are understood, is completely incompatible with the notion of an all-powerful and beneficent God. The contradiction was neatly and famously put by Epicurus the Greek philosopher of *ataraxia*, peace and freedom from fear, and *aponia* – the absence of pain. He wrote, 'Either God wants to abolish evil, and cannot; or he can, but does not want to. If he wants to, but cannot, he is impotent. If he can, but does not want to, he is wicked. If God can abolish evil, and God really wants to do it, why then is there evil in the world?' Either God lacks power and is therefore not omnipotent, or he lacks compassion, is merciless and therefore not omnibenevolent. To resort to a God-hypothesis when confronted by evil and suffering is, thus, a fantasy, an invention designed to offer strength and comfort. The atheistic alternative is a Godless world in which human beings are confronted with the brutal realism of a morally neutral and purposeless universe in which random happenings play out their effects on everything that lives.

This aspect of the debate represents totally opposed views of nature. Natural theology attempts to prove the existence of God from premises derived from the observation of the ordinary courses of nature. Paul, in his letter to the Romans, wrote, 'Ever since the creation of the world his invisible nature, namely his eternal power and deity, has been clearly perceived in the things that have been made'

(Romans 1:20). The problem has always been that the created world is itself a source of so much suffering. The atheist's alternative to natural theology is natural science, a process that demands we face 'the things that have been made' with a mind free of fancy and superstition. Rather than seeing in it God's 'invisible nature' we see nature itself which, in Tennyson's poem *In Memoriam A. H. H.*, is 'red in tooth and claw, With ravine shriek'd against his [God's] creed.' This stark, unsentimental perception of nature, offers no answer to the problem of suffering and evil, but faces us with the fact that, regardless of our fate, what we know is founded on the sure ground of experience and reason. Thus armed, we can accept that things are as they are.

Tennyson's poem asks the question 'Are God and nature then at strife, that nature lends such evil dreams?' It was noted above that, in their defence of God, theists have resorted to a theodicy. In constructing his theodicy, Leibniz argued that God could have created many different kinds of worlds but has chosen to create 'the best of all possible worlds', and that we can see what features such a world would contain. Leibniz was a mathematician and unsurprisingly argued that the axioms built into creation ought to have provided laws that operated consistently and economically. Leibniz called the principle by which God created 'the principle of the best', or 'the principle of sufficient reason'. Evil exists because in God's scheme it is an ingredient of the best of all possible worlds; it is not something to be denied or rationalized but something to be accepted as an element necessarily co-existing with good. The two need each other. It is in this necessary tension between good and evil that humanity exercises its free will, an important subject we will return to in Chapter 7. The paradox is that we have free will in a deterministic universe held together by the inviolable consistency of the laws by which it operates. Our free will is therefore exercised only within the parameters set by those laws. For God to improve on this situation would risk impairing the world in other, more significant ways, such as reducing the scope and sense of the free will we have so that we become mere puppets whose strings are manipulated by natural law. The theodicy suggests that God goes along with evil, that he 'allows' it as part of the best possible worlds. Jung, in *Answer to Job*, suggests that evil is the 'dark side of God'.

It seems theists must settle for evil and suffering in this world, while pinning their hopes for the next on the promise of Revelation 21:4, 'He will wipe away every tear from their eyes, and death shall be no more, neither shall there be mourning nor crying nor pain any more, for the former things have passed away.'

However, it is worthwhile to look briefly at two biblical accounts of suffering and, ironically, the 'message' here is also of relevance to atheists. The first is the account of the suffering servant as given by the prophet Isaiah, 'He was despised and rejected by men; a man of sorrows, and acquainted with grief. Surely he has borne our griefs and carried our sorrows . . .' (Isaiah 53:3–4). The 'suffering servant' is a typology that carries through to the New Testament as a prefiguring of Jesus' suffering on the cross. It is an image deeply etched on Western culture by the art and music it has inspired, such as Bach's Passions and Handel's 'Messiah', and the countless paintings and sculptures given over to this subject. The second image is that of Job whose suffering was so extreme that he cursed the day he was born, 'Why did I not die at birth, come forth from the womb and expire?' (Job 3:11).

If we combine Isaiah's prophecy of the vicarious suffering of the servant, with the existential suffering of Job, we have a poignant image of the problem. The response of both these men to suffering is their acceptance of it. In response to losing his entire family and all his possessions Job says, 'The Lord gave, and the Lord has taken away; blessed be the name of the Lord' (Job 1:21), and he asks, 'Shall we receive good at the hand of God, and shall we not receive evil?' (Job 2:10), When faced with crucifixion, Jesus asked to be relieved of the 'cup' of suffering, 'Abba, Father, all things are possible to thee; remove this cup from me.' But again, there is the acceptance, 'yet not what I will, but what thou wilt' (Mark 14:36). Both Job and Jesus acknowledge that God has the power to stop or remove the cause of suffering and in both cases God 'chooses' not to. As hard as it is for a theodicy to reconcile the concept of a powerful and all-loving God with our experience of evil and suffering, the ability to accept the suffering suggests the reason for it, a reason as relevant to atheists as to theists, that in the best of all possible worlds, we can do no more than make the best of it. Whether or not we subscribe to the God-hypothesis, suffering and the experience of suffering are part of our evolution and contribute to our unfolding. Atheists are left with the need to accept suffering as a fact of life and to draw on their courage and resilience. Theists will also draw on these attributes but are also faced with reconciling suffering and evil with a world believed to be created by a benevolent God.

Atheists pin all their hopes on this one world and on the one life we have in it, and to come to terms with and understand the problem of suffering, they have turned to personal and social psychology. Ernest Becker suggested in his important book *Escape from Evil* that 'the historical importance of psychoanalysis is precisely that it has revealed to us the dynamics of human misery'. In giving a psychologist's account of the problem that straddles the spiritual–secular boundary, Becker cites Otto Rank, Wilhelm Reich and Carl Jung. Put briefly, these three very different thinkers find their own way to a similar conclusion: we suffer because in the aftermath of Darwin and the scientific revolution we refuse to face up to the fact that we are animals. Religious doctrine has planted the idea that, by virtue of having a soul, we are the crown of God's creation, and that in the hierarchy of the life of this planet we are its lords. Religion has also beguiled us with the idea of immortality, a notion that makes a radical distinction between humans and other animals. On the other hand, the philosophy of the Enlightenment, driven as it is by reason, has conditioned us to believe that, in every way, but especially intellectually, we are superior to all other forms of life. In Nietzsche's term, we are the *Übermensch,* the Overman, or the 'Above-human'. We absorb these ideas because this distances us from the truth we try to avoid, that we are animals who live with a sense of our own mortality, the denial of which is itself the cause of much suffering. These, then, are 'the dynamics of human misery'. Rank's assertion that we fear both life and death; Reich's belief that we have contrived a culture that cushions us from facing our own mortality; Jung's assertion that the psyche of every human being has its own 'shadow', the mark of our inferiority and imperfection, our fear of life passing and of our impending death. These psychological insights leave little or no place for God; it is an analysis which, when placed alongside that of physicists and evolutionary scientists, provides a sober view of reality. There is more to be told, however, and the story continues in Chapter 7.

On the basis of the foregoing, the view of atheism is that religion, in any form, is dangerous and detrimental to society to the point where Christopher Hitchens declared that it 'poisons everything'. Religion, he insisted, is totalitarian in principle and is, of necessity, authoritarian, dogmatic and prejudiced. Furthermore, there is a correlation between religious fundamentalism and dangerously extreme right-wing politics. Belief in God, and the commitment to religion, serves ulterior interests of the kind history has recorded, such as the 'Holy Wars' of the Crusades, the Inquisitions' uncompromising protection of theological orthodoxy against heresy, the trial of witches, the subversion of scientific truth, the destruction of cultures by missionaries and, in our time, the driving fundamentalism and fanatical motives behind terrorist attacks. Theists reply that countries that have legislated for atheism, such as the Revolutionary France's 'Reign of Terror', with it's anti-clericalism, Stalin's Russia and Mao's Cultural Revolution China, have no better human rights record. However, this kind of knock-for-knock exchange does not advance the argument.

As well as the major themes discussed above, atheism's view of religion focuses on many other issues which can only be referred to briefly.

i)   There is the problem of theists claiming that the religion to which they are committed is the one true faith and that it represents a monopoly of truth, if not the entire truth. Thousands of years into religion, these faiths are still in violent conflict both among and themselves and with each other.

ii)   As we have seen, not only do concepts of God change, religions and faiths also come and go. The Greek and Roman gods are the fascinating subjects of mythologies and histories, and their shrines are now museums. The same is true of the gods of Norse mythology, indeed, the gods of all mythologies.

iii)   As with gods, so also have false messiahs appeared and disappeared; the 17th century gave us Sabbatai Zevi, the 18th century, Jacob Joseph Frank, and the 20th century, David Koresh and George Baker, otherwise known as

'Father Divine'. The ephemerality of religion gainsays the claim both for relevance and permanence.

iv)   Atheists also claim that religion is illusory, thus all that is claimed to be derived from it is illusory, that it represents a form of mental illness or delusion, that it is a social construction devised by the primitive mind to aid survival, and that as such it represents an immature stage of human development.

v)   More serious is the charge of 'child abuse', an emotive term proposed in this context by Richard Dawkins and Christopher Hitchens, who point out that children are vulnerable to religious teaching because it induces fear, guilt, and prejudice against science and reason. Both of these writers are echoing the philosopher Arthur Schopenhauer, who wrote in *On Religion: A Dialogue*, 'If, in early childhood, certain fundamental views and doctrines are paraded with unusual solemnity, and an air of the greatest earnestness never before visible in anything else; if, at the same time, the possibility of a doubt about them be completely passed over, or touched upon only to indicate that doubt is the first step to eternal perdition, the resulting impression will be so deep that, as a rule, that is, in almost every case, doubt about them will be almost as impossible as doubt about one's own existence.'

This overview of atheism's complaints against religion is far from complete. Theists have naturally responded, and their counter arguments will be considered subsequently.

Chapter Five

Experience

WHATEVER KIND OF EXPERIENCE a religious experience is, it is clearly different from all other forms of experience. What is an experience? What is happening when we have one, and how do we receive and process it? For convenience, the discussion falls under the following headings: the Nature of Experience; Religious Experience; Language and Experience; and the Way of Religious Experience.

1. The Nature of Experience

The word 'experience' has entered our language from the Greek *emperia*, via the Latin *experientia*. The orthodox view of experience is of something entirely associated with the senses, and Empiricism is that branch of philosophy that focuses exclusively on sense experience. Knowledge gained in this way is contrasted with knowledge that is only theoretical, although the latter may lead to the former. Rationalism, in contradistinction to Empiricism, holds generally to the view that all our knowledge is acquired by reason, and Aquinas' Five Ways, his arguments for the existence of God outlined earlier, are examples of arguments that are based on reason.

While the relationship between reason and knowledge is clear, the relationship between knowledge and experience, whether in a place of worship or a laboratory, has never been satisfactorily established. We proceed on the principle that everyone has experiences all the time, every moment of every day, even during the night in the form of dreams. Experiences are the common coinage of our lives; we absorb them, share them, seek them, avoid them, try to forget them, recall them, record them but mostly take them for granted. We do not pause at every moment to register this continuous flow of experience, which is a large part, if not the entire part of our conscious lives. There will always be experiences that are unprecedented, exceptional, horrific, ecstatic, life-affirming and life-denying, and these we remember, but for the most part our experiences flow past us like the proverbial water under the bridge.

This is an important part of the discussion, because it concerns the central question of how we know things. Led by philosophers like John Locke and David Hume, Empiricism developed as a reaction to another school of thought, 'Idealism', the theory that what we know of the external world is created by the mind. Idealists are quite happy to accept that material things, matters of fact, exist in the normal way, but they argue that while they exist they are not independent of our minds. The various forms of Idealism are associated with the philosophers promoting them. George Berkeley, for example, in denying the existence of material substance, believed that the objects we see, such as cups and saucers, trees and rocks, are only ideas in the minds of those who perceive them. He put it trenchantly, 'to be is to be perceived'. Our perceptions reside within us. Thus if we say that a bird is black and white, we do so only because we perceive it in that way. The argument led to what Kant termed 'transcendental idealism', the notion that whatever exists in space and time does so only according to appearance, and has no existence other than in our thoughts. The argument rests on the theory that, at birth, the human mind is already equipped with concepts and ideas that owe nothing to experience.

Since these ideas allow for the kind of knowledge derived from metaphysics and religious perceptions, Idealism is a philosophy that is comfortable with the God-hypothesis. Empiricism, on the other hand, can lead to atheism since it denies that anything can be known to exist outside of our physical senses. Hume, for instance, although he remained ambiguous on the subject of the existence of God, had to defend himself against the charge of atheism since he did not believe in the God of traditional theism, a concept he held to be incompatible with sense experience.

Empiricism was able to plead its case against the background of the emerging scientific revolution which, by means of experiment and the testing of hypotheses, set the standard for objective, verifiable knowledge. That we can be confident of the truth of such knowledge seemed to vindicate the argument that only what we learn through the senses is reliable. Empiricism has thus always been a stronghold for atheists. In his book *Physics and Philosophy*, Sir James Jeans defined science as, 'the earnest attempt to set in order the facts of experience'. The problem with an argument based on this kind of experience, is that knowledge is acquired slowly and progressively. In this process many things believed to be true have eventually been found to be wrong, thus empirical knowledge is endlessly self-correcting. It is also limited by its own terms of reference, by what the current state of science makes accessible, and by what, at any given time, are the accepted criteria for demonstrating that something is true. Even allowing for these limitations, Empiricism has always remained sceptical about the more holistic claims of Idealism and the metaphysical systems it supports.

From these two broadly opposed views of knowledge and how it is acquired, we need to look more closely at what might be termed subjective experience. If the argument for the God-hypothesis is to gain ground, it needs to be able to demonstrate and validate what is claimed when an appeal to an experience of God is made. A distinction has also to be made between conscious experience and self-conscious experience, and in order to be more objective in evaluating the validity of our experience, we need to look carefully at the question as to whether a world might exist that is independent of 'my' own experience. Underlying all of these themes is the nagging question of the validity of any experience that remains subjective, and how its validity might be demonstrated. It can be suggested that a person with an experience is never at the mercy of a person with an argument. It is a comforting and reassuring assertion, and in one sense it is workable. You can hold your argument-besieged experience within you, confident that the experience was valid for you. But it does not help with the problem of how to talk about the experience in a way that enables someone else to share and understand it or, if challenged, how to vindicate the truth claimed for that experience. If there is no wish, or necessity, to share the experience, if it remains personal, the problem does not exist. But if the claimed truth of the experience is to be communicated to others, or held to be true over against opposed opinions, it requires validation.

Philosophers and psychologists have long argued about the extent to which all experience is subjective and self-conscious. Some, such as the contemporary Danish philosopher Dan Zahavi, claim that every experience is relative to the 'I' that is experiencing it, and thus every experience is a self-conscious experience; others, such as Dr Joseph K Schear of Oxford University, challenge the idea that conscious experience entails self-consciousness. Clearly, every experience is 'my' experience, even that of the scientist looking through a microscope or telescope; 'my' experience is a private experience and, as mentioned above, if it remains so, there is no problem. The fallacy is to make the jump from the private to the public domain, for example, claiming that an experience of God, in the personal, subjective sense, is ground for claiming knowledge of a universal, creator-God as an absolute truth. It is this kind of experienced-based claim that Richard Dawkins dismisses as delusory and wish-fulfilling. Freud, in *The Future of an Illusion*, expressed a similar thought, 'We call a belief an illusion when a wish fulfilment is a prominent factor in its motivation and in doing so we disregard its relations to reality, just as the illusion itself sets no store by verification.'

Jung, while identifying himself with the scientific attitude and method, acknowledged his debt to his own religious experiences which are recorded in his *Memories, Dreams, and Reflections*. His private, subjective God-hypothesis was unconventional and he admitted that 'they would have burned me as heretic in the Middle Ages!' Jung's concept of God is a big subject. It is necessary to understand that he believed the process of psychoanalysis was an integral part of religion, to the point where his entire system of analytic psychology has been thought of as another religion. Put briefly, Jung believed God to be the 'collective unconscious', and because of this God is in-dwelling in everyone's personal unconscious. Heidegger, in his *Letter on Humanism*, points out the problems of both the private and public domains, 'Man', he writes, 'must recognise the seductions of the public realm as well as the impotence of the private.'

All forms of experience put together a kaleidoscope of impressions, feelings, and images, that form the individual's perspective of the world from one, particular, point of view. But even in the sharing of a common experience, individuals will differ markedly in how that experience is registered and understood. The differences between people's experiences do not have to be as clear and extreme as those of the theist and atheist in order for us to realise that with regard to most experiences we can only imagine the extent to which they are shared. Two people can share the same experience of an object or an animal, or of another human being; agreement can be reached that the object, a ball, is round and yellow, that the animal, a dog, has a head, four legs and a tail, that the human being is female, tall, and wears exotic clothes and jewellery. What is shared is mutually recognized data, although in analysis it might be found that the two perceptions differ considerably in detail. What cannot be shared is the 'wholeness' of experience itself, what the sight of the object, the animal or the human being means to the other.

The extent to which we believe the experience we share is actually the same experience is something we assume on the basis of having had similar, previous experiences and that the knowledge so derived is also similar. This 'sharing' is something we do most of the time; we compare our experiences and assess them against the experiences of others. In this way, we may reach a better understanding of our differences, but we may also establish common ground. We assume roundness and yellowness are properties so common that we all have the same perception of them; the properties of a dog are more complex but again we assume a shared experience on the authority of data accumulated from earlier experiences; the properties of a human being are even more complex, but we seek for, and establish, the common ground on which our experiences of others are based. That we are human ourselves provides us with a whole range of information which contributes to that experience. An aesthetic experience, for example, of the theatre, an art exhibition, a concert, is fraught with problems when looking for common ground on which to share it. Such moments are subject to differences of opinion, emotional responses, matters of taste, to the point where it might seem that the only thing we have truly shared is the time spent looking at whatever the object was. Moving on from this to sharing abstract experiences, those we experience in terms of thought, feelings, imagination and intuition, heightens the problem. Everyone assumes they know what is meant by beauty, love, joy, grief, fear and anger, and in daily life we assume we have enough 'experience' of these in common to make the sharing meaningful. But we also realise that in such circumstances all we can know is that the other person is appreciating beauty, or is suffering, or is happy or frightened. Even when experiences are shared, they are *different* experiences of the *same* thing and, if that is so, to what extent can it be claimed that they are the same thing?

Our attempts to share experience are based entirely on the assumption that what we hold to be true of our own experience we believe, or assume, to be true of other peoples'. Thus, the constant flow of our personal, subjective experiences are, at the same time, part of the common stock of other people's objective world, in that everyone recognizes we all have experiences that are subjective. When I try to tell someone about an experience I've had I have to describe it, and this is usually done by using spoken or written words, but in that process the person in question is also having an experience of me explaining what I want to explain while, at the same time, relating my point of view to their own experience. Maureen Gamble, a lecturer in psychology and sociology at Wichita State University, summed up the issue in her article 'Psychology and Experience' by pointing out that, 'reality, that ultimate test of objectivity, may only be an individual subjective experience created by our participation and observation. Our collective reality may be constructed and rearranged by our thought, intentions and expectation.' We live all of the time in the tension between subject and object, subjectivity and objectivity, and this dualism, as we shall see, is of central importance when it comes to religious language and experience.

The discussion turns us back to the question that has become the central point of the subject: how valid is my point of view? What can I know with confidence? Even in science, there is both doubt and certainty, a subject referred to by the zoologist J Z Young in his 1950 Reith Lectures. Professor Young made it clear that when pressed to explain something scientists show 'uncertainty, doubt and confusion'. The atheist claims to be able to demonstrate the validity of the case against God; theists argue that the objectivity of scientific experience is something that is assumed, and that scientists hold to their claims to 'truth' even though they know that it is both relative and temporary. Atheists, in their turn, argue that what are offered as proofs of the existence of God are only vague ideas based on mythology, fantasy and the kind of incommunicable subjective experiences referred to above. The response of theists is to point out that atheists misunderstand the nature of religious experience and that, while they accept that no worthwhile philosophy would reject the facts established by science, scientific atheism assumes that it is somehow exempt from philosophical scrutiny. Professor H J Paton made this point in *The Modern Predicament*: 'Scientists have no more right than theologians to claim immunity from philosophical questioning . . . Some scientific thinkers, anxious to get rid of knowledge altogether, reduce experience and thinking to mere behaviour, or mere talk.'

Before we consider religious experience itself, there are two more elements to be added to this general survey of experience, imagination and intuition. In *Cosmic Religion*, Einstein wrote, 'I believe in intuition and inspiration. Imagination is more important than knowledge. For knowledge is limited whereas imagination embraces the entire world, stimulating progress, giving birth to evolution. It is, strictly speaking, a real factor in scientific research.' To what extent, then, are imagination and intuition relevant for validating the God-hypothesis? Imagination is usually held to be distinct from those processes of cognitive and rational thought by which knowledge is normally acquired. An imaginative person is thought to be creative in a free-rolling way to the point where what is already known is rearranged, or reordered to form original ideas and perceptions. To put this another way, imagination is a faculty that enables a person to construct out of sense-impressions the image of something not present, or an idea that is entirely new.

Philosophers vary in their response to the way imagination functions. For Plato it was a primal or proto-cognitive faculty illustrated by the prisoners in his analogy of the cave, all of whom imagined it be their entire world, and the shadows cast on the cave wall to be real people. In Plato's account of this, Socrates imagines a group of people who have spent their entire lives chained to the wall of a cave. They spend their time watching shadows cast on to the wall of the cave by a fire and they begin to give these shadows forms and patterns. The suggestion is that these shadows are as near as the prisoners will ever get to reality.

In contrast Kant, in *Prolegomena to Any Future Metaphysics,* somewhat surprisingly took imagination to be the condition of all possible knowledge since it combines or synthesizes the functions of the mind. In Kant's words it is 'the act of putting different representations together, and of grasping what is manifold in them in one knowledge'. Imagination here is a unifying power that enables us to see relationships between otherwise disparate experiences and to gain knowledge from this synthesis. Other philosophers, such as Schiller, Schopenhauer and Hegel, also held that imagination was indispensable to knowledge.

Jean-Paul Sartre argued that imagination conditioned much of what we term 'consciousness'. In *The Imaginary: A Phenomenological Psychology of the Imagination*, he made an important distinction between imagination and perception, arguing that perception, by definition, is dependent on observation while imagination is not. For example, when we see a house we can, at any given moment, only see it from a particular point of view, but if we imagine a house we can see every part of it at once and wander around it both inside and outside. What Sartre tells us we imagine is a 'melange of past impressions and recent knowledge'. For Sartre, the imagination is the guarantee of our freedom, an idea developed in *Being and Nothingness*. He makes the interesting and important point that if we were incapable of imagining possibilities, if we couldn't perceive the unprecedented, we would be restricted to what is 'real', factual and empirically verifiable. Everything in which our experiences engages us has imaginative potential.

What is central to all of these various views of imagination is memory. The synthesizing power of imagination holds together different aspect of our acquired knowledge by drawing on what is stored in our memories. While imagination draws on memory, it is not confined to it. It can reorder what is remembered so as to construct something entirely new, but it can also envisage something new that is suggested by present observations, reflections and their possibilities. What we imagine is world-related and constitutes part of what we intend for the world and for our own lives.

What Kant wrote about imagination and synthesis carries through to his thoughts on intuition. In much the same way he argued for the synthesis of concepts and intuition: 'concepts without intuitions are empty, intuitions without concepts are blind'. Intuition figures large in discussions about how we acquire knowledge and is often referred to as a sixth sense, the 'sense of intuition'. Knowledge gained by this sense is uninferred and sometimes thought of as immediate knowledge, or perception, a kind of 'penny-dropping' experience. Philosophers have indicated several areas in which we may have intuitive knowledge; relevant to the theists' case is our knowledge of ineffable objects or concepts, such as time, space and God. Theists argue that intuition can give rise to an awareness and knowledge of God, an awareness supported by an intuitive trust in our own experience. It is what the American psychologist Carl Rogers called 'intuitive sensing', something that the seeker of knowledge carries to all the processes of learning. 'Intuitive sensing' is as important to science as to metaphysics and leading scientists from Kepler to Einstein have had to trust it. The problem remains that whatever is intuitively sensed in religious terms remains subjective. But, as Jung explained in *Psychology and Religion: West and East,* we do not 'make' or contrive our intuitions, they are insights that just happen, they come to us, or dawn on us; we have a hunch about something, then set out to see if it has any real substance.

Although the God debate focuses on Western religions, specifically Christianity, the discussion will need to be carried to Eastern religions which have a very different view of God, reality, experience, intuition and so on. The *Tibetan Book of the Dead* tells us, 'The mind is of intuitive wisdom.' For Tibetan Buddhism, mind is related to the capacity for immediate awareness, a concept familiar to followers of the Zen practice of meditation. Whether what we are made aware of is God, or a nameless, ultimate reality, the perception is the sum total of our previous experience refined by intuition. In this context, atheists argue that intuitive wisdom is more concerned with possibilities than with facts. For them, intuition is not a tool that will establish something as a fact, it is a kind of sixth sense, or a gut reaction, something they accept as a faculty or function of the mind that might lead to further, more rational enquiry.

2. Religious Experience

A religious experience is different from all other forms of experience. The argument for the God-hypothesis based on experience is probably the most telling and important for theists, but it is also the most questionable and easily refuted by atheists. As we have seen, such experience remains subjective and incapable of validation. Religious experience has a very long history and it is so universal and wide-ranging in its varieties that it is difficult to concede that all of them are based on a delusion. Can so many have been so wrong for so long? We can hear the atheists cry, 'Yes!'

As we have seen, one of the problems of religious experience is how to communicate it. It needs to be described, but how can that be done? Even if words can be found, the words themselves offer no basis for recognizing the truth with which they are concerned. Perhaps because of the difficulty of the task many religious people hold back from trying to explain their experience. What words can explain is its content in theological and doctrinal terms, but they do not describe the experience itself. Religious language is notoriously ambiguous, dealing with meaning by inference and metaphor. Unfortunately, many claiming religious experience hide behind the mystery of it, as if the experience, impressive and profound, is made real by virtue of it being irrational and beyond the comprehension of those who have not had it. Often, what is put across as religious experience is deliberately made to sound secret and esoteric, suggesting that the enquirer has no chance at all of understanding it without passing through some form of initiation.

In his book *Religious Language*, Ian Ramsey throws down the gauntlet for those who try to say something about their religious experiences, 'What can be said can be said plainly. It if cannot be said plainly, we should be suspicious of its claim to be said at all.' However, there is a place for what Ramsey calls 'odd language', something that features in all disciplines. Given that the God-hypothesis is unusual in drawing on experiences that are not thought to be 'normal', it should come as no surprise that theists use unusual words, including the word 'God' itself. But scientists also use unusual expressions in trying to describe their own concepts, for example Newton's 'absolute space', and Hoyle's 'continuous creation'. The problem of language, as we will see, is made more complex by the fact that each discipline has its own specialized language, and because it uses that language to serve its own purpose. For example, the theologian, the scientist, the philosopher, all use language differently according to their particular needs. The language used by religious people is inclined to be poetic; it is charged with the 'feelings' of religion and is expressive of worship, intercession, awe, joy, need and much else. The language of theologians is descriptive; it endeavours to encapsulate ideas about religion and the religious life in a systematic way which tends towards dogma, if not dogmatism; the language is formal and intellectual. Science, of course, has its own languages. Its statements are made by mathematics, formulas and the matrices of various computer programmes. There are constant discoveries of new materials, objects and concepts; these have to be named and to begin with their names and descriptions are known only to those using them. But with the popularization of science, many of these terms, such as atom, quark, proton, neutron, and their definitions, have become part of our common language as have the names for newly discovered or constructed materials, such as nylon or Teflon. Philosophy uses many different kinds of language; it can be speculative, analytic, rigorously logical, or it can revert to what philosophy calls the 'linguistic method', the analysis of language itself as a means of understanding how it is acquired, developed and used. That said, theists argue, with some point, that no language can adequately express any experience it tries to describe.

3. Language and Experience

Given the problems of language in communicating religious experience, it is interesting to look at some of the attempts made to explain or describe such an experience. Firstly, within the Christian tradition.

In *The Confessions*, St Augustine wrote: 'Thou hast called, Thou hast cried out, and hast pierced my deafness. Thou hast enlightened, Thou hast shone forth, and my blindness is dispelled. I have tasted Thee, and am hungry of Thee. Thou hast touched me, and I am afire with the desire of thy embraces.' In his book *The Spiritual Canticles*, the 16th-century Spanish mystic, St John of the Cross, spoke of the quietude of religious experience: 'God teaches the soul very quietly and secretly, without its knowing how, without the sound of words, and without help of any bodily or spiritual faculty, in silence and quietude, in darkness to all sensory and natural things.' St Teresa of Avila describes the overwhelming visions that came to her. She sustained intense visions for a period of two years, among which was one of a seraph that pierced her heart with a golden, fiery lance: 'I saw in his hand a long spear of gold, and at the iron's point there seemed to be a little fire. He appeared to me to be thrusting it at times into my heart, and to pierce my very entrails; when he drew it out, he seemed to draw them out also, and to leave me all on fire with a great love of God. The pain was so great that it made me moan;

and yet so surpassing was the sweetness of this excessive pain, that I could not wish to be rid of it.' John Wesley, in *Mr Wesley's Conversion*, recorded that, 'In the evening I went very unwillingly to a society in Aldersgate Street, where one was reading "Luther's preface to the Epistle to the Romans". About a quarter before nine, while he was describing the change which God works in the heart through faith in Christ, I felt my heart strangely warmed. I felt I did trust in Christ, Christ alone, for salvation; and an assurance was given me that he had taken away my sins, even mine, and saved me from the law of sin and death . . . But it was not long before the enemy suggested, "This cannot be faith; for where is thy joy?" After my return home, I was much buffeted with temptations; but cried out, and they fled away. They returned again and again. I often lifted up my eyes, and he sent me help from his holy place. And herein I found the difference between this and my former state chiefly consisted. I was striving, yea, fighting with all my might under the law, as well as under grace; but then I was sometimes, if not often, conquered: now I was always conqueror.' C S Lewis became an atheist at the age of fifteen. In *Surprised by Joy*, he said he was 'very angry with God for not existing'. He confessed to being brought to Christianity like a prodigal, 'kicking, struggling, resentful . . . You must picture me alone in that room in Magdalen night after night, feeling, whenever my mind lifted even for a second from my work, the steady, unrelenting approach of Him whom I so earnestly desired not to meet. That which I greatly feared had at last come upon me. In the Trinity Term of 1929 I gave in, and admitted that God was God, and knelt and prayed: perhaps, that night, the most dejected and reluctant convert in all England.'

Judaism is predominantly a religion of right practice in which religious experience is not easy to isolate, since for the majority of Jews the seeking and worship of God is mostly a communal affair of the synagogue and the family. The Kabbalah, Judaism's principal mystical tradition, is complex and esoteric but offers a vivid insight into the kind of language used to describe the personal experience under discussion. Abraham Abulafia, the founder, in the 13th century, of the school of 'Prophetic Kabbalah', explained to his pupils what to expect in seeking God: 'Your entire body will then begin to tremble, and all your limbs will be seized with shuddering. You will experience the terror of God, and will be enveloped with fear of Him. You will then feel as if an additional spirit is within you, arousing you and strengthening you, passing through your entire body and giving you pleasure. It will seem as if you have been anointed with perfumed oil from head to foot. You will rejoice and have great pleasure. You will experience trembling for the soul and trembling for the body . . . The Divine Presence will then rest on you.'

Such extreme physical manifestations of a religious experience are found within many religions, but in Judaism 'experience' is more usually embedded in the practice of the religion rather than in its contemplation, and in the rigorous observation of law. The Jew is more likely to cast his eyes downwards rather than upwards, but orthopraxy, the correctness of religious conduct and practice, cultivates a form of spirituality termed, in Hebrew *halakhah,* 'the way'. In a religion so given to practice, the language used of religious experience is more mundane, the poetry and imagery left for the Psalmist. The American orthodox Rabbi Joseph Soloveitchik, a Talmudist and philosopher, has written an account of *halakhah* in his book *Halakhic Man,* in which he becomes passionate about religious experience which springs from tradition: 'The chain of tradition will continue until the end of time. . . . This wondrous chain . . . represents the manner in which the

Jewish people experience their own history . . . There can
be no death and expiration among the company of the
sages of tradition. Eternity and immortality reign here in
unbounded fashion. Both past and future become, in such
circumstance, ever-present realities.'

(Compare Chapter 3.2 Arguments from History.)

In Islam religious experiences are rooted in 'signs' given
by Allah. The Qur'an (45:3–5) is clear that, 'in the heavens
and the earth are signs for those who believe. And in your
creation, and all the wild creatures He has scattered over
the earth, are signs for a people of firm faith. And the
alternation of night and day, and the sustenance that God
sends down from the sky, quickening thereby the earth
after her death, and the ordering of the winds – these are
signs for a people who understand.'

Somewhat like Judaism, the deeper experiences of the
religion are linked to right practice, such as fasting, alms-
giving, and the observation of the five daily periods of
prayer with their ritual ablutions. A Muslim, even if just
once in his life, will try to make the hajj, the pilgrimage
to Mecca. It is in an addition of these practices that the
devout believer will experience the thrall of his faith.

Alongside this orthopraxy lies a rich tradition of Islamic
mysticism which calls on recognizing and responding to
'signs within the self', as well as to the external signs.
The records of Islamic mystical experience all speak of
something intense, ineffable and inexplicable, an experience
which seems expulsive of everything that is not God. It is
described by the Sufi poet Mansur Al-Hallaj: 'Thy Spirit
is mingled in my spirit even as wine is mingled with pure
water. When anything touches Thee, it touches me. Lo, in
every case Thou art I!'

The language used by mystics to describe their experiences suggests that, regardless of the markedly different
religious traditions in which they are sourced, they share

experiences in common. Whether Jewish, Christian or Islamic, they speak of a unity with the divine to the point of there being no difference between their own essence and that of God. All of the above accounts are of profound and life-changing religious experiences within various scriptural traditions. Whatever the detractors of the God-hypothesis have to say about this, what is professed is an experience, and the experience itself is real. Its origins however, must remain a matter of interpretation.

For a more complete account we need to consider religious experience in non-theistic traditions. The examples that follow are taken from records of the experiences of Zen Buddhists who have gained *kensho* or *satori*, that is, enlightenment, from within a tradition that is rigorously non-dualistic. While what is experienced is not thought of as God, it is nevertheless, a religious experience.

In *An Introduction to Zen Buddhism,* D T Suzuki explains that the Zen experience of *satori* 'is an experience which no amount of explanation or argument can make communicable to others unless the latter themselves had it previously ... When a man's mind is matured for *satori* it tumbles over one everywhere. An inarticulate sound, an unintelligent remark, a blooming flower, or a trivial incident such as stumbling, is the condition or occasion that will open his mind to *satori*.' In the Zen tradition, such an experience is thought of as 'immediate perception', a concept referred to before. There are degrees of enlightenment in the sense that the practitioner can experience anything from passing glimpses of the 'truth' or 'reality', to a complete perception of it.

Despite the problems of trying to explain and communicate the experience of *satori*, Roshi Philip Kapleau, in *The Three Pillars of Zen,* records the attempts made by those trying to describe their experience of enlightenment.

The first example is of a young woman called Yaeko Iwasaki, who wrote to her teacher, the celebrated Sōtō Zen monk Sogaku Harada-Rōshi, about her enlightenment: 'I have seen my face before my parents were born clearer than a diamond in the palm of my hand. The absolute truth of every word of the patriarchs and the sutras has appeared before my eyes with crystal clarity . . . My world has been revolutionised.' Mr K Y is a Japanese business executive: 'I came to realise clearly that Mind is no other than mountains, rivers, and the great wide earth, the sun and the moon and the stars . . . Then all at once I was struck as though by lightning, and the next instant heaven and earth crumbled and disappeared. Instantaneously, like surging waves, a tremendous delight welled up in me, a veritable hurricane of delight . . .' Mr K T, a Japanese garden designer, in trying to describe experience, wrote: 'Just in front of my knees I saw a large post and the leg of a small table overlapping. At that moment I felt the post to be the roshi [old teacher, or master] and the small leg to be myself. Suddenly this insight came to me: The post as a post is occupying all of heaven and earth, and the leg of the table as the leg of the table is doing the same. The Roshi as Roshi and I as I fill the entire cosmos. Is there emptiness anywhere? With that I laughed heartily from the bottom of my belly.' Mr A K, a Japanese insurance adjuster: 'My mind was as empty as an infant's as I listened to the roshi's lecture. He was reading from an ancient koan [a paradoxical phrase or verse posing a question that cannot be solved by reason]: "Not even a sage can impart a word about the Realm of Silence from which thoughts issue . . . no, not even a Buddha." "Of course, of course!" I repeated breathlessly. "Then why have *I* been searching for such a word?" All at once everything became sheer brilliance, and I saw and knew that I am the only One in the whole universe! Yes, I am that only One!'

It is not really possible to make a valid comparison between the dualistic God-based religious experience of biblical religions, and the non-dualistic, non-theistic experiences of the kind found within Eastern religions. However, in broad terms it can be said in summary that for theists religious experience means an encounter with God which, understood anthropomorphically, is analogous to our meeting with other people in the immediate, objective world. To this basic encounter with God, religions attach a wide range of theologies that ascribe to God various attributes such as omniscience, omnipotence and others of the kind already discussed. This 'encounter' is understood in terms of a meeting and, thus, a relationship. The relationship can be so intense that the sense of the loss of self becomes an experience of absorption or mingling with the essence of the divine nature. In the second case, where the experience is non-theistic but which, nevertheless, is an intense and real experience, 'encounter' is probably not the best word to use, since there is nothing to be 'met with', no one, or nothing with which to have a relationship. What seems to be experienced is a perception of, or sudden insight into, the essential oneness and unity of all things. It is an 'enlightenment' or an 'awakening', a realization that seeing the world as an addition of separate objects is illusory, a fundamental error in the way we think and, therefore, in the way we acquire knowledge and understand the knowledge acquired. In experiencing a transcendence of duality there is nothing that necessarily rests on a belief in the existence of God, and atheists seem not to have taken fully into account the implications of non-theistic religious experiences.

4. The Way of Religious Experience

At this point, it is useful to look more closely at the different ways in which people have come to a religious experience. The following headings are for convenience and none of them are, in themselves, exclusive and the different modes of experience may overlap or combine.

The way of the numinous

Rudolf Otto's book *The Idea of the Holy* edges the God-debate towards a concept theists and some atheists might share, that is the feeling or sense of 'something other'. The book offers both psychological insight into religious experience and an enquiry into the nature of religious language. Nevertheless, the experience Otto analyses is of a transcendent reality, the aspect of religious experience that is non-rational. Normally, we say an experience is non-rational if we can sense or feel it but are unable to conceive it or express it in intelligible language. For example, we can conceive of God as an Ultimate Being, as Creator or a Spirit, as the Life Force or Love. We can hold to any of these without being conventionally religious, or we can attach theologies and doctrines to them. A commitment to a religious institution such as a church or mosque, or to an intellectual concept such as a creator God, is not what Otto understands as 'true religion'. For this, he argues, there must be something 'other', an experience of what he terms 'a unique original feeling-response', that is not in any way dependent on the rational elements of religion and their attached theologies. The word Otto uses to define this feeling-response is 'numinous', and it is this, he claims, that is uniquely characteristic of religious experience: 'There is no religion in which it [the numinous] does not live as the real innermost core and without it no religion would be worthy of the name.' He also uses the term '*mysterium tremendum et fascinans'*, meaning 'fearful and fascinating mystery', what today is popularly termed 'awesome'. It is this that is the object of the numinous.

When Otto uses the term 'numinous', it is to focus precisely on that aspect of experience that is not caused by or dependent on doctrine or theology or a moral idea. Any experience of the numinous will be entirely original since no two people's experience of it will be the same. The numinous, Otto explains, has always been, and will always be there, even though not recognized as such. Through the experience of the numinous, Otto argues, it is possible to apprehend the existence of the object that inspired it. But the concept is not inevitably religious. Detractors of the God-hypothesis, such as Dawkins, Hitchens and Sagan, argue that our sense of the numinous is not dependent on the supernatural and has to be separated from it. That separation, however, might only be slight. Atheists experience the numinous in the form of intense pleasure, or rapturous joy, or an overwhelming aesthetic response, or a sublime moral elation, and these experiences may be of the same character as our sense of the *mysterium tremens*, since the source of the experience remains something of a mystery. Theists do not always call the object or source of such experiences 'God', which is to say that while they are not credited to God, they may still be experiences that address ultimate meaning. Because an experience of the numinous tends towards the irrational, and because it transcends objective reality but is, nevertheless, an experience atheists may share, they need to take a close look at their attempt to distinguish the numinous from the metaphysical.

The way of the mystics

From the examples of the experiences of mystics given previously, it seems that their path is the way of negation, that is, they arrive at an experience of God by self-discipline which leads to self-denial, then to self-emptying. In Eastern tradition this means an emptying of the mind so as to take in, or realize everything. Such an experience comes very close to that of the Western mystics, as Meister Eckhart affirmed in one of his sermons, 'to be full of things is to be empty of God. To be empty of things is to be full of God.' The question arising is, does the emptying of the mind, a concept not easily understood in the West, lead to a clearer or immediate perception of a reality beyond 'normal' experience? Since the mystics' experiences are personal and subjective, the question can only be answered by them, and only they can judge their validity. As Professor Paton put it, 'the experience itself is the guarantee of truth, and their conviction of its validity is absolute'. Thus, while the question of validity is not a problem for the mystic, it remains so for the atheist who wrongly assumes that the mystical encounter with God is analogous to that of one human being to another. The atheist cannot sustain a debate about the existence of God, or an experience of God that is cast in the kind of language used by mystics; endeavouring to do so using language drawn from the way human beings relate to each other fails to address the nature of mystical experience. (See 'The way of relationship', below.) Atheists, therefore, are inclined to dismiss the whole mystical experience as a form of self-hypnosis akin to a state of trance. Interestingly, it is through mystical experience that the believer abandons anthropomorphic language and finally overcomes the traditional dualisms, the great divide between the individual self and the absolute or universal being. Such differences between theists and atheists may, again, be a problem of language. In debating the existence of God, ironically, it is the atheists who seem to be restricted by anthropomorphic language.

The way of revelation

The experience and the knowledge thought to be given by revelation presupposes a revealer, and this concept is the founding principle of biblical religion and the primary means of gaining a knowledge of God. Revelation can be both progressive and instant, general and personal. It is progressive in the sense that the biblical religions believe revelation began with creation but continues on from it; it is the Psalmist's 'The heavens are telling the glory of God; and the firmament proclaims his handiwork' (Psalm 19:1), and it is Paul's 'Ever since the creation of the world his invisible nature, namely, his eternal power and deity, has been clearly perceived in the things that have been made' (Romans 1:20). The experience of revelation can be personal and also instant, as for example when Moses received God's laws on Sinai, or the way in which the prophet Jeremiah was given authority to speak for God, 'Then the Lord put forth his hand and touched my mouth; and the Lord said to me, "Behold I have put my words in your mouth"' (Jeremiah 1:9). The immediacy of revelation is graphically illustrated by the conversion of Paul while travelling to Damascus, 'Now as he journeyed he approached Damascus, and suddenly a light from heaven flashed about him. And he fell to the ground . . .' (Acts 9:3–4).

Revelation is a disclosure given from without but apprehended within the subject, a distinction important when we come to consider 'realization'. Furthermore, the revelation arises entirely from God's, that is, the revealer's, initiative. Although records of revelatory events have persisted down the years, such as miracles, appearances or hearing voices, the authority of such an experience rests entirely with the individual in question and offers no proof that would convince anyone who has not had a similar experience. Kant wrote against revelation as an argument for the existence of God: 'conviction of God's existence can come from reason alone, not from either inspiration or any tidings, however great their authority'. The only bridge that might be built between the concept of biblical revelation and reason is one of shared purpose: both are trying to describe the nature of reality.

What emerges from a revelatory experience is that it is life-changing; anyone who has been the recipient of revelation is one person before it happens and another immediately afterwards. Even atheists would have to admit that something has taken place, something has happened. What brings about the change is far more than special knowledge, although that will be a consequence of it; the transformation is made by an encounter with a power, an emanation, a presence, or sense of something fundamental. This returns us to Otto's 'numinous' and to the *mysterium tremendum*. A revelatory experience is something that cannot be ignored, it demands response and significantly we only know about the revelation because of the response that is made to it.

It can be argued that the consequences of God's self-disclosure, the subject's responses to it, are what make revelation what it is. By dismissing the concept of revelation as the communication of something that has no content, atheism misses the point. Revelation always has content, but it is more of a side-effect; the content is the reason for the revelation, such as a commission to undertake a particular task or to carry a message. But from the subject's point of view, what is 'given' is the event, the happening of God's self-disclosing presence. Thus, the validity of this kind of experience is to be found in the subject's response to it, and in the transformation this brings about in the life of that person.

The way of realization

If revelation of, for example, God or the absolute, is an experience thrust on the subject from outside by a revealer, then realization of, say, ultimate truth, can be thought of as being drawn from within the subject by their own volition and focused practice. Eastern traditions tell us that we carry, within ourselves, all that we need in order to know the ultimate truth which may, or may not be referred to as 'God'. The implication of realization is that we are, in a sense, independent, that we don't have to rely on anything 'given' for an experience of the Ultimate. The truth about reality resides within everyone and the only means of developing its potential is through certain disciplines such as meditation or contemplation. Self-realization is the goal of ancient, esoteric Eastern practices that have spread throughout the West through the influence of movements such as the Self-Realisation Fellowship, founded in America in 1935 by Paramahansa Yogananda. The practices have also become familiar through New Age belief systems. These are concerned with the realization of one's true or essential self, and what this leads to is generally described as an experience of a conscious and personal sense of unity with everything. As described above, such systems can lead to a negation, to the apprehension of 'nothingness', an experience equally accessible to atheists as to theists.

Realization is also a form of enlightenment which is the word often used to translate the Sanskrit term *bodhi*, literally meaning 'awakened'. The Japanese words *satori* and *kensho* were referred to above; the actual awakening, or the 'immediate perception' of truth is the experience of *sunyata*, or emptiness. But this is not nihilistic, since it is an experience of 'something' even though that something is beyond conception or description. This emptiness is clearly non-theistic, something that in one sense cannot finally be experienced by a subject, since in the process of enlightenment the subject is dissolved in the emptiness. It is, in other words, the Buddhist equivalent of that kind of loss of self experienced by Christian mystics. The difference is that not only is the awareness of self lost, but so also is that sense of dualism implied by experiencing union with another. Another element has to be added to the concept of realization, namely that its experience is not separate from the world of phenomena, nor is it either absolute or relative. The oneness is total. In his book *The Foundations of Tibetan Mysticism*, Lama Govinda explained that, 'The relationship of form and emptiness cannot be conceived as a state of mutually exclusive opposites, but only as two aspects of the same reality, which co-exist and are in continual cooperation.' This relational balance is confirmed by one of Buddhism's central texts, *The Heart Sutra*, 'Form is emptiness and emptiness is indeed form. Emptiness is not different from form, form is not different from emptiness. What form is, that is emptiness, what is emptiness, that is form.' Put simply, there are not two or multiple worlds, all is one.

What this contributes to the debate is the idea that the physical and metaphysical are not necessarily mutually exclusive or in opposition, they can and may need to relate to each other in a kind of perceptual symbiosis. A similar relationship may be found between natural law and spiritual intuition, the former relating to physical forces and the latter to a sense of harmony and order immanent in them. The closing of the gap between the physical and metaphysical is well summarized in *The Tao of Physics* by Fritjof Capra: 'The field theories of modern physics force us to abandon the classical distinction between material particles and the void. Einstein's field theory of gravity and quantum field theory both show that particles cannot be separated from the space surrounding them.' This does not, of course, advance the argument for the God-hypothesis, but it does advance the possibility that the findings of modern physics may make an important contribution to the process of realization or enlightenment and, thus, to the debate.

The way of relationship

The argument for the existence of God has traditionally been dependent on how we understand what it is to be a person, a human being in relationship to other human beings. All religious anthropomorphisms are based on this. There is something of ultimate meaning and value to be found in the way we recognize and address one another, especially when this gives rise to a sense of true mutuality. Evolutionary biologists understand the human species to be a very advanced form of an earlier and more primitive progenitor, a proto-human species. Even the subtlest of our faculties, those concerned with aesthetics and morality, our ability to imagine and reflect, to remember, to choose, to hold and develop abstract concepts, are all centred in the brain and have a physical source. The mind is a function of the brain, while the notion of the soul, or the psyche that combines both mind and soul, are dismissed by atheists as illusory. Even though the concept is not necessarily dependent on the God-hypothesis, atheists dismiss the concept of a soul, or the possibility that there is any aspect of personal consciousness that will survive death. All traditional religion stands against this view, even those religions, like Buddhism and Taoism, which are non-theistic. Certainly the concept of resurrection on the Christian model is difficult to sustain, but there are grounds for keeping an open mind about reincarnation, as we shall note in Chapter 7.2

Primarily, through the influence of the movement in philosophy known as Existentialism, some weight has been given to the idea that if God exists he does so primarily 'in relation', and can be best encountered within our relationships with each other, or as Buber put it between the 'I' and the 'Thou'. We can only treat Buber's ideas briefly. His philosophy is based around the concept of relationships represented by the primary words 'I', 'Thou' and 'It'. From these three fundamental relationships emerge: the I–It relationship which is our relationship with objects, the I–Thou, relationship which is our relationship with other people, and the I–Eternal Thou relationship, which is our relationship with God. Buber argues that the 'Thou' of the other person may be perceived and experienced in ultimate terms: we can perceive God in each other as the Eternal Thou and, as such, God is to be encountered in our relationship with other people. While Buber is concerned with the meaning of our relationship with everything, the heart of the matter is our encounter with other people; he claims that 'All real living is meeting.'

What Buber is contributing to the God debate is a philosophical anthropology that understands that each one of us can perceive the Eternal Thou in another person. In our relationships with each other a new being comes into existence, or rather, the ever-existing and indwelling Being can be experienced in relationship. In *I and Thou*, Buber puts it this way: 'The aim of relation is relation's own being, that is, contact with the *Thou*. For through contact with every *Thou* we are stirred with a breath of the *Thou*, that is, of eternal life.'

These brief paragraphs do not do justice to the rich and complex fabric of Buber's thought, and we are left with the basic problem of how we perceive ourselves and each other, and what value we give to the other person. The strength of Buber's argument lies in the fact that what 'truth' may represent is to be found within ourselves; if that truth reaches for something metaphysical then it does so in existentialist terms, that is it starts where we are and reasons outwards to something 'other'. Buber is not a mystic, he is not saying that in perceiving God in each other anything is transcended. It is simply that in our relationships, rightly understood and conducted, something of ultimate value and meaning is disclosed, namely the Eternal Thou. This, for Buber, is God.

In this survey of experience a number of conflicting, theist–atheist issues have emerged that touch on different concepts of both the nature and structure of experience, and of religious experience in particular. This raises questions about how we can judge the validity of the experiences we have, to which various disciplines such as philosophy, philosophical theology, psychology and anthropology make their distinctive contributions.

Firstly, the debaters needs to consider the question as to whether religious experience is something special and exclusive, something apart and out of the ordinary, and the extent to which the claims can be validated. Secondly, the question arises as to what criteria are used to distinguish between an experience deemed to be religious and one that is secular. Thirdly, how are we to understand the terms 'religious' and 'spiritual' when applied, for example, to moral and aesthetic experiences. Fourthly, more thought, even perhaps a reappraisal, needs to be given by both parties with regard to the origin or source of religious experience in terms of both individual and collective psychology, and fifthly, in the light of the discussion on realization and relationship, whether religious experience is something that transcends consciousness, or whether, as atheists would claim, such experiences are entirely subjective and self-generated.

Those arguing against the God-hypothesis have picked up the problem that religious experiences can conflict, that between the wide variety of such experience there may be no common ground and that schisms and wars have been fought over these differences, heretics burned, the saints of one religion regarded as the apostates of another. Theists need to respond to the question that if all these various and sometimes opposed experiences are claimed to be religious, can all of them be valid? Can there be more than one ultimate truth, or is there only one, underlying truth? These themes will be discussed in Chapter 8.

Chapter Six

Faith, Reason and Knowledge –
Their Relationship and Authority

'WHAT INDEED HAS ATHENS to do with Jerusalem?' asked the early Christian author and apologist Tertullian. It is a question about the relation between reason, here represented by Athens, and faith, represented by Jerusalem. Whether or not the kind of knowledge acquired by faith is as valid as that deduced by reason is one of the most hotly contested themes of the God-debate, and one with which contemporary philosophers of religion still struggle. Faith is the essential attribute, or faculty, required by those who support the God-hypothesis; to believe in God and to have any knowledge of God is to be grounded in faith. Atheists dispute the argument that faith alone can validate the claims made for religious experience, demanding further, empirical confirmation of the kind used by science. However, the psychiatrist Wilhelm Reich claimed that 'scientific theory is a contrived foothold in the chaos of living phenomena'. Scientists, of course, while disputing that their foothold on reality is contrived, make the same criticism of faith, arguing strongly that it is a wish-fulfilled position improvised by those who believe in God, to substantiate as real, knowledge and experience that scientists hold to be entirely delusional.

Both theists and atheists use the words 'belief', 'faith' and 'knowledge' loosely, and it is useful to clarify the distinctions. Atheists take belief to mean that what is held to be true is conjectural, something that is not completely substantiated by observation or experiment. It is commonly used to suggest trust, as in 'I believe in the pilot' or 'I believe in you.' For the believer, to say that something is 'believed in' implies that it is true, even though it cannot be proved. Generally, in religion, to say 'I believe' (for example, as in the Apostles' creed, 'I believe in God the Father Almighty, Maker of heaven and earth . . .') is to acknowledge the real existence of the object of belief. Since this belief is not founded on knowledge in the usual sense, the basis for the belief is faith. The problem arises, as we have seen, when the content of 'belief in' is taken to be 'knowledge of' in an empirical sense, and when faith, in the absence of something more demonstrable, is understood as validating that belief. In the New Testament, the terms 'faith' and 'belief' are frequently taken to have the same meaning; for example, Mark 9:24, 'Lord, I believe, help Thou my unbelief.' Also, both words are taken to be synonyms in common usage.

As this aspect of the discussion develops, we shall see that the arguments of the debate are between i) faith and reason, and ii) knowledge and belief. Generally, theists acknowledge that pure reason cannot prove or disprove the existence of God, because the subject goes beyond reason's terms of reference. The sad history of religious evangelism has left a record of people compelled to conversion, some- times by torture, but no one can be compelled to faith. If faith is embraced, it can only be so by free choice. The long list of martyrs include 'heretics' who have chosen to die, not for the sake of their religion but for the sake of their faith. The distinction here, between 'religion' and 'faith', is important. A martyr may die, not for the sake of Christianity per se, but because his faith and, thus, his conscience, does not enable him to believe in, for example, the doctrine of the Trinity. Atheists reply that even those who are prepared to die for their faith have had to put their reason aside for the sake of it. Atheists assert that between the stand of faith and that of reason is a basic irreconcilability. This, however, would be disputed by Jewish, Christian and Islamic martyrs, many of whom in dying for their faith, believed they had good reason to do so.

What is faith? While the concept was always to be seen, shadow-like, in the developing theologies of Christianity, it took the Luther-led Reformation to liberate faith as a ground for religious belief. Hitherto, Catholicism had defined faith as 'the acceptance of a statement on authority'. Access to the Church and to God was governed by ritual and effected by baptism, a sacrament believed to ensure the eternal life of the subject regardless of the strength of faith or the moral quality of that life. 'Justification by faith', the leitmotif of the Reformation, together with the availability of the Bible in the lingua franca of mid-Europeans, set people free to search for a personal God in a personal way. Faith and the content of faith thus became subjective and linked to perception and intuition, to feelings and emotions. In one sense, the story of the emancipation of faith is the story of the emergence of personal religion as an alternative to mere conformity to the authority of a received tradition, whether it be that of Church or synagogue (among others). Interestingly, this idea of the liberating effect of real faith was a theme taken up by St Augustine of Hippo, who wrote in *The City of God,* 'Love God and do what you like.' It is a precept that, while being loosely interpreted, has been used to challenge traditionally held beliefs. Typical was the stand taken by Martin Luther: 'I cannot and will not recant anything, for to go against conscience is neither right nor safe. Here I stand, I can do no other, so help me God. Amen.'

(I return later to the crucial implications of personal religion.)

Perhaps the most famous definition of faith is that given by Paul in Chapter 11 of his Letter to the Hebrews, 'Now faith is the assurance of things hoped for, the conviction of things not seen', and Paul continues throughout this longish chapter by illustrating the concept of faith from events in Old Testament history, such as 'by faith Abraham, when he was tested, offered up Isaac', and 'by faith the people crossed the Red Sea as if on dry land'. Paul only stops because he claims he has no more time to tell the full story of faith. Here, the term 'faith' implies trust and confidence in the truth of something that has been enacted, an intervention by God taken to be an actual historical event. The basis of faith is, thus, made objective by placing it on something outside the believer, centred on events that have been made significant because God is believed to have intervened in them. It is faith in God having so acted, that he has directly involved himself in human affairs, that is the basis for the argument for the existence of God from history.

For most believers, however, even though they have faith in an absolute truth, the faith itself is never quite absolute. William James understood that, 'Faith means belief in something concerning which doubt is theoretically possible,' and doubt always seems to have been faith's shadow. Paul Tillich thought that doubt and faith were not necessarily in conflict: 'Doubt isn't the opposite of faith, it is an element of faith.' Atheists tend, sometimes, to misunderstand the concept and function of faith, because they assume a declaration of faith is offered as proof of the existence of the object of that faith. However, there are few, if any, believers who would offer their faith in God as proof of God's existence. Blaise Pascal observed that 'Faith is different from proof; the latter is human, the former is a gift from God.'

If Pascal is right, and faith is a gift from God, then many people seeking the truth, even atheists curious enough to let themselves be open to the possibility of faith, are going to be disappointed. There are traditions which claim that faith is limited to a 'chosen' few, such as the Jehovah's Witnesses who believe that exactly 144,000 will be taken up to Heaven. The number is doubtless symbolic, like the 40 days and nights of Noah's flood, or that same period of time spent by Jesus in the wilderness. However, limiting those gifted with faith to a specific number (or limiting them in any other way) involves the contentious principle of selection. Whether or not faith is something gifted by God, it can be argued, as does Rudolf Otto, that there are people with a special religious faculty, which he calls 'the faculty of divination'; but this, in turn, seems to admit to some form of spiritual privilege.

Kierkegaard's notion of how a person might come to believe in God has passed into popular usage as 'a leap of faith'. He compares true religious faith with romantic love, but argues that in both cases there will never be enough evidence to justify total commitment in the sense of giving yourself unconditionally to the other. This complete giving over of oneself, Kierkegaard suggests, cannot be done on the strength of evidence but only by that 'leap of faith'. Importantly, he was also persuaded that such an abandoned commitment required faith and doubt to be combined, doubt being the rational, commonsensical component of religious belief. He argued that doubt is a quality of faith and that, if unaccompanied by doubt, faith – for example in the divinity of Jesus – would be mere credulousness. He noted in his *Journals* that 'doubt is conquered by faith, just as it is faith which has brought doubt into the world'. Kierkegaard's point is that faith and doubt are inextricably related, that once faith is established, doubt will be a fellow traveller, but that to move from doubt to belief requires the 'leap of faith'.

Against this brief overview of faith, the obverse question must be put, what is reason? This question, which has been running below the surface of the previous chapters, has a wide range of answers since the word 'reason' is used in many different contexts. For example, it can refer to the cause, justification or explanation of something, or, in logic, as the premise of an argument supporting a belief. More generally, reason, that is, 'reasoning', is used to specify the thinking function of the mind, the capacity to understand, the ability to make logical judgements, to argue, and to discriminate in the process of evaluating or judging something, and in solving problems. To be reasonable is to act in accordance with common sense, while 'to reason' is to persuade with rational argument. For the purposes of the God-debate, the atheist lobby sets reason, not only against faith but also against concepts such as imagination, experience and emotion. Reason itself is neutral; it is a means of arriving at the truth of something objectively. The actual process of reasoning can be inferred from the different ideas and forms of argument offered, but its conclusions can be observed directly in the choices people make and the way they behave in response to those choices. As expressed by the atheist philosopher of religion Anthony Flew: 'We have no independent road to acquaintance with the Goddess of Reason.'

(But see Chapter 8 for an account of Flew's move from atheism to religious belief.)

Aristotle defined human beings as 'rational animals' and argued that the highest happiness and well-being is achievable only by a life constantly lived in accordance with reason. The theme carries through to modern philosophy – for example, to Descartes who rejected the traditional spiritual world-view that understood human beings to be animals endowed by God with reason, in favour of regarding them as 'thinking things', with 'thinking' as the function that distinguishes us from anything else in nature, animals included. What a human being is, for Descartes, was defined by the faculty of thought. In his *Second Meditation*, he wrote that, 'At this time I admit nothing that is not necessarily true. I am therefore precisely nothing but a thinking thing; that is a mind, or intellect, or understanding, or reason – words of whose meaning I was previously ignorant.' He was moving towards his famous assertion 'I think, therefore I am', with its consequential body–mind dualism, and his concept of soul.

There have always been attempts to bring reason to bear on religion, and Chapter 3 included a review of the contribution to this by St Thomas Aquinas in his proposals arguing for the existence of God. In Chapter 2, it was noted how Kant argued that, to understand the premises of religion, we should not analyse metaphysical notions of reality but the way we think about them, and the structure of those thoughts. He was asserting, especially for religion, that what is significant is not the metaphysical world-view itself but the way those who perceive such a reality think and talk about it. This prefigures Ludwig Wittgenstein who, in a different context, argued that if you want to know what a word means to people, don't resort to a dictionary but consider how it is used by them. Modern philosophy, under the guidance of, for example, Wittgenstein and A J Ayer, moved us further along this road to the point of focusing on an analysis of language and meaning. In his *Culture and Value*, Wittgenstein suggested that religious discourse has become what he termed a 'language game', in which language is used very specifically to make certain kinds of statements which do not have, or need, any justification outside of themselves. What this linguistically analytic method has contributed to the debate about religion is to free it from the necessity to rework the old, somewhat worn-out concepts of God and the classical proofs for God's existence. The language in which these concepts have been expressed can now be subjected to analysis, not with regard to its intrinsic meaning but, on the Wittgensteinian principle, that it will be best understood from the way people use it. Linguistic analysis is a form of objective reasoning that allows the debate to reconsider what faith actually means for the lives of those who hold to a religious belief. It is not a subject that has been sufficiently considered by the anti-God party, and we will return to it in Chapter 8.

Against this brief overview of faith, reason and knowledge, two frequently recurring themes of the debate can now be considered.

1. Faith and Reason

In his *Large Catechism*, Martin Luther declared that 'all the articles of our Christian belief are, when considered rationally, just as impossible and mendacious and preposterous. Faith, however, is completely abreast of the situation. It grips reason by the throat and strangles the beast.' It is this kind of anti-rational stance that is the target of the scathing attacks on religion by critics such as Richard Dawkins, Christopher Hitchens and others. In *The God Delusion*, Dawkins writes, 'Faith is an evil precisely because it requires no justification and brooks no argument,' and when used as the ground for belief in, or knowledge of, something for which there is no evidence, faith, he says, 'is the principal vice of any religion'. In *God is not Great*, Hitchens asserts, 'Faith of that sort [of Aquinas or Maimonides] that can stand up, at least for a while, in a confrontation with reason – is now impossible.' Hitchens is saying that, faced with the new science's debunking of religion, no one today can hold to an irrational view and expect to be taken seriously. In *God's Undertaker: Has Science Buried God?*, John Lennox challenges Dawkins's assertion that all religious faith is blind, and he puts the question, 'Where is the evidence that religious faith is not based on evidence?' Faith and evidence, Lennox argues, are inseparable, and no one holding to a faith has ever suggested there is no evidence or reason for doing so. However, for Lennox, and presumably for others, that 'evidence' amounts to the received tradition of Christianity, itself based on the acceptance of historical events that have had religious significance laid over them – for example, in the accounts of miracles and the resurrection of Jesus of Nazareth. These 'events' amount to reasons for holding to a faith, but reasons are not evidence. What is accepted as evidence by the believer may not be accepted by scientists, but the tenets of faith, as Lennox and other scientists remind us, are not scientific propositions: they neither call on nor require empirical proof. Terry Eagleton, the literary theorist and critic, suggests an alternative view when he puts the case for God in *Reason, Faith and Revolution*. He argues that faith and reason are not antithetical, that 'religion needs to be patiently deciphered, not arrogantly repudiated. It springs from a realm to which reason should be no stranger.' He makes the point that no attack on religion made simply on the grounds of rational argument can be expected to succeed.

The tension between faith and reason has always existed, but a brave attempt to ease it was made by the medieval Franciscan philosopher William Ockham, who combined a profound and sincere commitment to God with a form of ruthless logic which seems strikingly modern and which enabled him to make distinctions that many contemporary atheists fail to do. Ockham was able to accept that while reason and experience could provide us with a knowledge of the physical world, they were incapable of leading us to a knowledge of God. In search for a knowledge of nature we must use reason, since all such knowledge is acquired through the senses. But a knowledge of God is not accessible to the senses, so we must use another, more appropriate faculty to gain it: namely, faith. Ockham's dualism, with nature and reason on the one hand, faith and God on the other, is creative in that it recognizes that different forms of knowledge are apprehended in different ways. Ironically, it can be said that the distinction Ockham made furthered the process of secularization because it set nature free from metaphysical assumptions and in so doing paved the way for the empirical sciences. In thus liberating the God-hypothesis from its traditional basis in natural theology, Ockham put himself at risk and he was recalled from teaching in Oxford to the then Papal seat at Avignon, where he faced charges of heresy.

The philosophical method for which Ockham is best known is based on the principle of parsimony or economy and is termed 'Ockham's razor,' a phrase that does not appear in his writings. The maxim it represents is: 'It is vain to do with more what can be done with fewer,' which is frequently represented as, 'Do not multiply entities beyond necessity.' In other words, if an idea, be it scientific, religious, or philosophical, can be understood without reference to a hypothetical entity, there is no need to assume it. Effectively, then, we should always opt for an explanation that stands on the fewest number of causes, facts or qualifications. In his *Mathematical Principles of Natural Philosophy*, Isaac Newton expressed a similar idea: 'We are to admit no more causes of natural things than such as are both true and sufficient to explain their appearances. Therefore, to the same natural effects we must, so far as possible, assign the same causes.' In applying this principle to the argument between faith and reason, Newton concluded that the simplest solution was to accept that faith and reason, rather than being in conflict, have their own distinct contributions to make to their respective disciplines.

In summary, Ockham asserted that there are different kinds of truths. A truth that is made real by faith is both ultimate and beyond our ability to understand rationally; a truth derived by means of science's observation of particular things, and their possible relation, is entirely rational and understood as being so. Put plainly, both Ockham and Newton appeal for simplicity, and subsequently there have been trends in philosophy and theology that have reduced original metaphysical complications to much simpler terms. The Reformation, for example, was in part concerned to do exactly this.

To apply the principle of Ockham's razor to the God-debate means that the hypothesis that God exists should be accepted if, in so doing, it helps to explain our existence and that of the universe in the simplest possible terms; if not, then atheism is the better option. Atheists contend that because there is no evidence for God's existence, the hypothesis requires a much more complex explanation, and Ockham's razor should be applied to the God-hypothesis.

While some theists argue that the proposition that God exists is the most intelligible and direct means of finding answers to the ultimate questions, others regard the principle of simplicity to be irrelevant. They are comfortable in accepting the irrationality of what they believe, knowing their belief to be dependent on something like Kierkegaard's 'leap of faith'. Ockham himself was a theist whose faith, within the context of his 14th-century culture, enabled him to harmonize faith, reason and experience with a belief in revelation through the Word of God. In his *Summa Logicae*, his manual of logic, he wrote: 'Only faith gives us access to theological truths. The ways of God are not open to reason, for God has freely chosen to create a world and establish a way of salvation within it apart from any necessary laws that human logic or rationality can uncover.'

This opposition of faith and reason remains one of the central themes of Western dualism. We have inherited what Richard Tarnas described as 'the psychological necessity of a double-truth dualism'. There have been many attempts in Western religious philosophy to reconcile this opposition, or to build a bridge between them, but none of them have been entirely successful. The German theologian Rudolf Bultmann set about reinterpreting the supernaturalism of Christianity by a process of 'demythologizing' the biblical texts. By expounding the New Testament in such a way as to free the text of the mythical world-view of the 1st century, Bultmann believed it would have greater relevance and appeal to people whose culture was rapidly being defined by science and technology. It was a process that might have appealed to some atheists. Dietrich Bonhoeffer, a German Lutheran pastor and theologian who was hanged by the Nazis for his involvement in a plot to assassinate Hitler, continued the process of reinterpretation and de-mythologizing by developing in his writings what he termed a 'religionless Christianity' that was more suitable to a 'world come of age'.

Paul Tillich also attempted to recast the concept of faith and its relationship to reason. In his book *The Courage to Be*, he wrote: 'Faith is not a state which appears besides other states of mind . . . It is the situation on the boundary of man's possibilities. It *is* [author's italics] this boundary.' It can be argued that both theists and atheists would be better walking this boundary together, rather than firing verbal bullets at each other across it. In *The Dynamics of Faith*, Tillich asserted that 'the dimension of faith is not the dimension of science, history, or psychology', and that some atheists misunderstand faith because they assume it addresses and relates to the world in the same way as does science. Tillich was making much the same point as is now being made by theistic scientists such as John Polkinghorne, that perceptions of faith are concerned with an area of knowledge unsuited to scientific enquiry. Tillich pointed out the irony that religious fundamentalists are as guilty of misinterpreting the relationship between faith and reason as are some atheists. For example, the fundamentalist view of Christianity is attacked by non-fundamentalist Christians exactly on these grounds, that the fundamentalists are thought to distort the religion they profess. The same tensions are found in both Judaism and Islam.

Faith, however, does not stand alone in its apprehension of God, since reason, Tillich argued, has a crucial role to play in the problem of ascertaining truth in religion; but he also says unequivocally that the truth, or the validity of a religious view, cannot be demonstrated by the kind of reason associated with the scientific attitude. It is only when we confine reason to this narrower, scientific sense that it becomes opposed to faith. In its broader use, reason is the *sine qua non* of what it means to be human, it is humanity's defining characteristic, and as such, faith must complement it. It is this, more general view of reason that critics of the God-hypothesis tend to neglect.

In *The Dynamics of Faith*, Tillich remarked on the extent to which atheism has been influenced by the French philosopher and founder of sociology Auguste Comte, who claimed that the sciences have superseded religion. Comte's thesis is that religion was the first attempt to understand, guide and direct human destiny, but that it failed to do so and lost ground, first to philosophy and, eventually, to science. Tillich held Comte's analysis to be wrong, since a distinction has to be made between religion and what he (Tillich) termed 'authentic faith'. While religion in its institutional forms might be concerned to guide and direct human destiny, he said, authentic religious faith can never be a means to an end, since it is an end in itself. What has lost ground, therefore, are the institutional and established *forms* of religion, not the energy of the faith that originally inspired them.

2. Knowledge and Belief

It was mentioned above that 'belief' and 'faith' are commonly used synonymously, and for the purposes of this section, so as to understand the implicit clash between knowledge and belief, it is not necessary to hold the two concepts rigidly apart – that is, we can allow that they mean something similar. However, belief is customarily taken to be the reason why an assertion is accepted as being true when not supported by clear evidence. In this sense, we may have faith in what we believe, or we believe something 'in good faith' because we have perceptions and experiences that enable us to do so. H J Paton, in *The Modern Predicament*, made the point that 'the predicament caused by the gulf between belief and knowledge is acute in the modern world, but is also very old'. The problem remains critical and strongly debated because philosophers have always been concerned to know how we can acquire knowledge in which we can be entirely confident. In the *Phaedo*, Plato has Simmias say: 'about such matters [the immortality of the soul, the afterlife, the mind and knowledge, etc.], it is either impossible or supremely difficult to acquire clear knowledge in our present lives. Yet, it is cowardly not to test in every way what we are told about them, or to give up before we are worn out with studying them from every point of view. For we ought to do one of the following things: either we should learn the truth about them from others; or we should find out for ourselves; or, if this is impossible, we should take what is at least the best human account of them, the one hardest to disprove . . .'

For purposes of the God-debate, Simmias' 'every point of view' implies that we must put together our concept of the world by using both knowledge and belief, since to use just one of them would result in a distorted and incomplete picture. Such distortions sustain the dualities engrained in Western philosophy and psychology, such as soul and body, mind and matter, reality and appearance, unity and plurality, eternal and temporal, divine and human, and we can add to this curriculum of dualism, belief and knowledge, science and religion, faith and reason. In attempting to bridge the gulf between these seemingly opposed concepts, Einstein famously said that 'Science without religion is lame, religion without science is blind.' For us, as well as Simmias, to 'acquire clear knowledge in our present lives' necessitates seeing and using the relationships between these apparent oppositions.

In *Reason, Faith and Revolution*, Terry Eagleton remarked that the relationship between belief and knowledge is complex. Belief can be rational, and history is full of rationally held beliefs, once assumed to be knowledge, that have subsequently been proved to be false, such as believing the Earth to be flat and that the Sun circled it because that was what it appeared to be doing. In both these cases, belief was taken to be knowledge, a confusion that had a profound influence on attitudes and culture. So entrenched were these misconceptions that when Galileo proposed in his *Dialogue Concerning the Two Chief World Systems*, an alternative perception of the Earth-centred solar system, he was put to trial by the Inquisition. Charged with heresy, he was forced to recant. The 'old, old story' prevailed then, and does so still in our own times – for example, in the prohibition of teaching Darwinian evolution in the schools of some American states. Today, science has shown that these traditional, sometimes fundamentalist beliefs are outmoded; to have relevance and meaning, they must be recast in such a way as to reconcile the concepts of knowledge and belief. Failure to do so can only lend strength to the atheists' arguments.

The previous chapter discussed the nature and authority of religious experience, indicating that a knowledge of or belief in God can be acquired in many different ways. In general, however, Simmias, a disciple of Socrates, offered good advice. Either we begin by acquiring a knowledge of God from others, or we 'find out for ourselves'; failing that, we resort to the best 'human account', or testimony. Many who believe in God have been set on their way by what they have learned from others. The knowledge gained of God, at least to begin with, was acquired because the person coming to belief was able to accept the validity of the other's claims. They had 'faith' in what they were told, especially, perhaps, if it was given by a 'specialist' such as a priest, rabbi or imam.

We live in an increasingly specialized world, and it is impossible for anyone, even those with prodigious general knowledge, to know something about everything, or even everything about one particular subject. We rely on the specialist knowledge of others to maintain our health, our cars, our homes, and to ensure the availability and quality of our food. If we want information about the origin and development of the universe and the life of this planet, we refer to astrophysicists and evolutionary biologists. So vast is the range of human knowledge that what any one of us might 'know' is a minute part of the whole. But when we listen to what the specialists have to tell us, we cannot, in every case, be sure that what they say is true, since we lack the necessary knowledge to make that judgement; yet because of the expert nature of their knowledge, we accept what the specialists tell us, we believe them to be correct. The nature of that belief, in relation to its content, illustrates the complexity of the concept of certainty, a complexity not sufficiently considered by some of the atheist rationalists. Theists participating in the current God-debate, whether they be theologians or scientists, claim that although knowledge of God is a particular form of knowledge, it is one accessible to anyone who makes a serious and focused attempt to acquire it.

Such is the nature of 'being religious', or better, perhaps, of evincing true spirituality, that the 'specialist' might well be a lay person, a friend, a member of the family, an adult or a child. What is important is that the religious specialist provides 'evidence' of their expertise in much the same way as does the garage mechanic, plumber or neurosurgeon. Such evidence can take many forms, such as a life that has clearly been transformed by religious experience, the depth of a person's compassion, their selflessness, their unconditional love. It is not at all suggested that all theists demonstrate these attributes, or that those who do have a monopoly of them, only that they are traditionally characterized and identified by them. When evidence of these graces, or 'fruits of the spirit', is apparent, thought needs to be given to the possibility that their source is, in some way, spiritual. Atheists rightly claim that altruism and love, in all their many forms, can be accounted for in other than religious terms. All forms of charity can have an entirely secular source and a humanitarian motive; but this does not exclude the possibility that they may also be driven by a religious energy. The thrust of the argument, however, is that to a greater or lesser extent we are dependent on other people for what we come to believe is true, and that the knowledge so derived is as valid for religion as for any other field of specialist enquiry.

As to Simmias' 'the best human account . . . the one hardest to disprove', this, for many believers, is the account given by history, especially with regard to the particular events of the kind earlier referred to and those listed by Paul in Hebrews 11. In Chapter 3, religious history, specifically biblical history, was considered as an argument for the existence of God. Here the purpose is to discuss religious history in terms of objective knowledge carried down to us through the passing of time. Belief has always been founded on the kind of knowledge embodied in history. In modern reinterpretations of the biblical texts, those for example of Bultmann referred to above, a distinction is made between the Jesus of history and the Christ of faith, and the making of that distinction has produced a library of books. Perhaps the most influential was *The Quest for the Historical Jesus* by Albert Schweitzer. This is not the place to develop what is a huge and controversial subject, but for the purposes of the God-debate the question needs to be asked: to what extent can we have sure knowledge of historical figures, such as Jesus or the Buddha, about whom claims have been made that have had momentous results and a definitive influence on the development of both Western and Eastern civilization?

The biblical religions are historical religions both in the sense that they are very ancient, with a long story attached to them, and because history itself is believed by these religions to be a vehicle through which God has disclosed his purposes for humanity. Extra-biblical but somewhat uncertain evidence for the historical Jesus was given by the 1st-century Jewish historian Josephus. Other sources, including four references in the Talmud, are alleged to refer to the life and death of Jesus of Nazareth. For example, in Sanhedrin 43a: 'It is taught: On the eve of Passover they hung Yeshu . . .'; and there is a letter by Mara bar Sarapion, who was neither Jewish nor Christian, written to his son from prison sometime between 73 CE and the 3rd century, in which reference is made to '. . . the Jews by the murder of the Wise King'. Such evidence is scant, but sufficient. However, the important point is the distinction made between the actual, historical Jesus and the Christ of faith with the claims made for him in the Christian creeds. While these are statements of belief, they are based on events presumed to be historical. The question of miracles and natural law will be considered in Chapter 7, but the claims that some historical events have lasting religious significance rest heavily on miracle and mythology.

H J Paton remarked that 'a religion in which a belief in historical facts is considered essential to faith may be called a historical religion'. But a distinction has to be made between facts that are historical and accounts of events written in such a way as to make them seem historical. This is being written at a time when the Jewish Passover coincides with the Christian Easter, itself a highly charged conjunction. The accounts of the plagues which God visited on the Egyptians to persuade Pharaoh to release the Hebrew slaves, the story of the angel of death 'passing over' the homes of the Hebrews rather than stopping by to kill their first born, the drama of the parting of the Red Sea to make a dry path for the fleeing Israelites, are celebrated every year as actual events. At Easter, Christians recall the crucifixion of Jesus of Nazareth, closely followed by his physical resurrection. The historicity of the crucifixion is probably secure, but that of the resurrection, despite the eyewitness accounts recorded in the gospels, is fixed as a belief-event that is the foundation of Christianity. The history may be ancient or very recent, it may be history in the making, but the tradition put together by an addition of events recorded over a long period may carry as many embedded truths, or untruths, as the history of science. The history cannot be ignored, either by theists or atheists, since what both claim as historical truths have been established, to paraphrase Bernard of Chartres, 'by standing on the shoulders of historical giants', such as Abraham, Jesus, Muhammad and the Buddha. The difference heightened by the debate is the competing understanding of history, the one side seeing it as sacred, the other as secular, but that it *is* history, both are agreed.

Whether or not a belief associated with a historical event constitutes knowledge may be a matter of how close that belief is to the event in question. The miraculous crossing of the Red Sea by the Israelites was, to them, a significant event in a way radically different from its significance to those who now celebrate the Passover. To have witnessed the resurrection – that is, to have been in the presence of the resurrected Christ, as were his apostles – is not the same as recalling the resurrection at Easter, however virile the faith that maintains belief in it. The difference is between living the event and remembering it, even if the act of remembering constitutes a present religious experience. Undoubtedly both these very distant events were totally transforming, the first for an entire people, the second for a very small group who represented Christianity in its infancy. What we have are exceptional, unprecedented events and their transforming power.

The Moroccan-born French philosopher Alain Badiou has developed a compelling philosophy in which he endeavours to include the concept, or idea, of 'event' into what he calls the 'science of being'. Badiou reasons that a person may find realization and reconciliation with truth in the place or function of the 'event'. In his *Being and Event: Philosophy in the Present*, a title echoing Heidegger's *Being and Time* and Sartre's *Being and Nothingness*, he writes that philosophy tells us: 'We must think the event. We must think the exception. We must know what we have to say about what is not ordinary. We must think the trans- formations of life.' Badiou is suggesting that the essence of truth, and our relationship with it, lies in the event itself, an event that is 'believed' to be God's intervention in human affairs. Faith in this belief is not a matter of acceding to the statements of a creed, nor can the belief be reduced to such a statement. As an atheist, Badiou understands faith to be a rigorous loyalty to the 'event', seen as an unprecedented happening completely out of line with, and incomprehensible to, the cultural context in which it occurred or is occurring. Eagleton's comment on this is: 'For Badiou, one becomes an authentic human subject, as opposed to a mere anonymous member of the biological species, through one's passionate allegiance to such revelation.' Eagleton refers to the old English word 'troth', which means both faith and truth, before which we are all equal, atheists and theists alike.

Another French philosopher, Jacques Lacan, suggested that if it happened that no religion were true, Christianity was more likely to have come closer to matters of truth than the others. The reason for this, Lacan argued, is that the essence of its truth is more directly related to the 'event' than in other religions. In short, as indicated at the beginning of this discussion, the foundation of the faith of an historical religion is formed by its central events. It is an important point, and one not duly considered by the anti-God argument that presumes religious truth is a matter of reflection and contemplation on an *idée fixe*, a mere proposition, or what Badiou calls, 'immobile knowledge'.

As we have seen, any discussion about knowledge and belief returns us to the question of how we can be sure that what we know is true, and whether what we believe (as opposed to what we know) is valid. In *God's Undertaker*, John Lennox suggests that science belongs to the public sector while belief in God belongs to the private sector. By 'private' Professor Lennox means personal. But for many followers of the various religions, the personal nature of belief must become public, and when it does, what is believed has to be communicated *as though* it was knowledge. This is especially important for those mandated to make their belief widely known – as are, for example, the more evangelical movements within Christianity, and Islam's requirement that Muslims must set out to convert the 'heathen'. In one sense, Lennox is right about the privacy of religious belief. Whether or not the believing community, be it of the Church or otherwise, is required to evangelize, there is a sense in which the individual's acquisition of belief, and the knowledge of God it brings, is a deeply personal affair. Even so, however deeply held a belief may be, the knowledge of God it leads to cannot be held to be 'knowledge' in the same sense in which we have knowledge, for example, of facts.

As mentioned previously, with reference to personal religion, it may be that the knowledge illuminated by genuine belief is so valid, so grounded in our personal being, that one of the most sensitive responses to it is silence. In his essay 'Can Religion be Discussed?', in Flew and Macintyre's *New Essays in Philosophical Theology*, the logician and philosopher A N Prior reduces the problem of talking about religion to the basics: 'Of course we can only talk nonsense when we talk about God . . . Of course the laws of thought, and the laws of grammar, forbid us to confess our faith – we try to speak of God, and it is impossible even to begin.' Although Prior continues by saying that God comes to our aid in the process of discussing religion, the essential ineffability of the subject seems to call us, finally, to privacy and silence.

The outcome is that, in matters of faith and its interaction with reason, knowledge and belief, there are some issues that are beyond expression; there is no adequate language, and there may be no adequate concept. The problem, as we have seen, arises only when we begin to give voice to faith, when we try to express the ineffable. But the same is true of empirical knowledge. Certain scientific concepts are so difficult to communicate and, thus, to understand, that those able to sign up to the rational 'creeds' that science discloses are members of a very small, esoteric group, akin to a secular cult. In a recent edition of *Scientific American*, it was reported that by computing telescopic observation of what can actually be seen, astronomers have calculated that there are more than 200,000 billion galaxies. Surprise was expressed that the number was so small. Such statistics, and their implications, are not the stuff associated with rational knowledge, and what they illustrate demonstrates the ineffability, not only of religious ideas but also of contemporary scientific concepts. We see here that, out on the edge of scientific knowledge and experiment, there are emerging concepts, perhaps 'mysteries', for which we have as yet neither words nor even reasonable concepts. In this sense, science shares with religion a lack of adequate language for perceptions, or theories, that remain beliefs in possibilities, rather than sure and certain knowledge.

Chapter Seven

Some Key Issues

IN PREVIOUS CHAPTERS, discussion of the God-debate has been about broad but central themes; the purpose now is to consider some specific, recurring subjects that are strongly disputed. While all the following are important concepts for the God-hypothesis, atheists take the view that ideas such as a belief in miracles and an afterlife are mere wish-fulfilling fantasies.

1. Miracles

In his book *A Mathematical Miscellany*, the Cambridge professor of mathematics James Littlewood defined a miracle as 'an exceptional *event* [emphasis added] of special significance occurring at a frequency of one in a million'. A person, he calculated, could expect this one-in-a-million event to happen to them at the rate of one per month. For Littlewood, it seemed, an event presumed to be miraculous was really commonplace. How nice it would be if this were true and we had the perception to recognize a miracle when we saw one.

All religions have accounts of miracles, but the biblical religions stand apart in that the faith they profess is dependent on them. Put simply, a miracle is an event that is not explicable by natural causes. From the Latin *mirari*, 'to wonder', such an event inspires awe because it cannot be accounted for by human or other natural means. The history of religion includes an extensive record of miracles taken to be manifestations of divine power consequent on a suspension of the laws of nature. The argument is that if God created the universe and life on this planet, then natural laws are a part of that creation and, if necessary, they can be suspended by the creator if it serves his purpose to do so. Biblical miracles, for example, have always been understood by those who believe in God as irrefutable proof of His existence; but it is not only God who works miracles – there is a long catalogue of saints who have performed, for example, miracles of healing. Potentially, anyone can perform a miracle. Matthew records Jesus as saying, 'For truly, I say to you, if you have faith as small as a grain of mustard seed, you will say to this mountain, "Move from here to there," and it will move; and nothing is impossible to you' (Matthew 17:20). Miracles, like faith itself, can be used to substantiate a special-case argument: to be able to perform a miracle, even to witness or be a subject of one, implies privilege. In 'A Moral Argument against Miracles' (*Faith and Philosophy*, Vol. 12, No. 1), Father James Keller wrote, 'The claim that God has worked a miracle implies that God has singled out certain persons for some benefit which many others do not receive, [and this] implies that God is unfair.'

In all discussions on miracles, a distinction has to be made between descriptive and prescriptive laws. Natural laws are descriptive: they are concepts that have been discovered by science and used to describe, or explain, how the universe behaves. Familiar examples include Newton's law of motion, which describes how solid objects behave when subjected to a force, and the fact that water at sea level will boil at a temperature of 212° Fahrenheit. Prescriptive laws, those constructed by society and which can be regarded as official rules, are designed to influence the way we behave; they determine the standards of our moral system. (See

'Ethics and Morality', below.) One of the most polarizing philosophical questions in Western culture is whether or not prescriptive laws are absolute or relative. Should the commandment 'You shall not kill' be applied in all circumstances, or are there times when to kill is necessary and justified? Generally, prescriptive laws are not fixed or absolute; they prescribe how a person 'ought' to behave. Contravention of prescriptive laws, therefore, is subject to the choices people make in observing the principles that regulate society, and infringement of these carries its own penalties. The ethical implications of prescriptive law for the God-hypothesis will be discussed later.

While there is nothing miraculous about the infringements of prescriptive laws, the assumed bending or breaking of scientific law is thought, by those who believe in God, to be a miracle of divine intervention. Theists have never argued that miracles dispense with natural law, or assumed that they conform to laws that are radically different, or suggested that they are of another realm or dimension as yet undiscovered by science. They recognize that any event that is understood as a miracle has to be dependent on natural law for it to happen. As the philosopher William Adams put it, 'A river must flow, before its stream can be interrupted.' When a miracle occurs – say, a miracle of healing – the physical laws no longer adequately describe the event. However, the matter is made more complicated because modern science – for example, the laws of quantum mechanics – have shown us that natural laws can contradict each other, but are still taken to be valid because of their consistent pattern. In his lecture in 1927 to the National Secular Society, Bertrand Russell referred to the contingency of natural law: 'We now find that a great many things we thought were Natural Laws are really human conventions. You know that even in the remotest depth of stellar space there are still three feet to a yard. That is, no doubt, a very remarkable fact, but you would hardly call it a law of nature.'

Since, by definition, a miracle cannot be regarded as having actually happened without recognizing that basic scientific principles have been suspended, scientists have abandoned any serious enquiry into their validity. For this reason, miracles have become a problem for proponents of the God-hypothesis. However, miracles occurred long before our present knowledge of physics, chemistry and mathematics, at times when how nature worked was still a matter of mystery and conjecture, and the question has to be asked, how were they then defined? Aquinas thought of a miracle as an event 'beyond the productive power of nature', where 'nature' includes ourselves. In his *Summa contra Gentiles*, he wrote, 'God is a cause that is completely hidden from us. Therefore, when some effect is wrought by Him outside the order of secondary causes known to us, it is called simply a miracle.' Aquinas uses the concept of the 'hidden God' in various contexts, for example in discussing the nature of faith and the way believers respond to the 'sense' of God – what Rudolf Otto was later to call 'the numinous'. Here Aquinas used the notion of the 'hidden God', not only to define what a miracle is, but also to comment on the nature of God. 'To act in this way, outside the order of secondary causes, is possible for God alone, who is the founder of this order and is not confined to it . . . so God alone can work miracles.' Aquinas distinguishes between three types of miracle: i) those worked by God directly, but which could never be done by nature alone, such as the account in Exodus of the burning bush, or in Joshua of God causing the sun and moon to stand still; ii) miracles worked by God *through* human agency, such as Jesus raising Lazarus from the dead, or the healing miracles of the saints; and iii) those worked through the agency of nature alone, but 'without the operation of the natural principle', for example, visions and 'appearances', or the miracle of the crop that grew a hundred times more than was sown (Luke 8:8). In all these cases, Aquinas assures us, 'they are rightly appealed to in proof of faith', that is, God's miracles support one's faith, or they can be referred to, or appealed to, as proof of faith.

In the modern period, the philosophical response to miracles was led by Hume who, in section 10 of *Enquiry Concerning Human Understanding*, argued that belief in a miracle can never be rationally justified. He called miracles 'a violation of the laws of nature'; thus, for Hume, belief in a miracle can only be based on faith in what are the causes of miracles. Generally, since Hume, philosophers have stepped back from considering the miraculous, regarding theology as the more suitable discipline. Supporters of the God-hypothesis, such as John Lennox and John Polkinghorne, both of whom are scientists, suggest that there are serious flaws in the arguments Hume put forward to support his dogmatic assertion that miracles are 'a violation of the laws of nature'. In the *Enquiry* referred to, Hume made his point clearly, 'That no testimony is sufficient to establish a miracle, unless the testimony be of such a kind that its falsehood would be more miraculous than the fact which it endeavours to establish.' This expresses the view of the New Atheists, who argue that the laws of nature are completely uniform or consistent, and that since we all live within the framework of those laws, our experience of them is also uniform or consistent. Hume dismisses miracles because they contradict the consistency of natural law, and because any experience of an event claimed to be a miracle is exceptional and thus undermines the consist-ency of our experience of such laws. The arguments against Hume question both these axioms, asserting that neither the laws of nature, nor our experience of them, are consistent or uniform. The grounds for questioning Hume are somewhat involved and covering them fully is beyond the scope of this book, but they can be summarized as follows:

i)   The consistency of natural law can only be argued from the possibility of inconsistency. In *God's Undertaker,* John Lennox points out that without irregularities it would not be possible to think of *laws* of nature at all. As he states, 'If nature is not uniform, then using the uniformity of nature as an argument against miracles is simply absurd.' Lennox is arguing that there are too many variations and anomalies in the laws of nature for it to be thought that nature operates with complete consistency. The argument for 'uniformity in nature' also implies, as mentioned above, the uniformity of experience. To illustrate this, Lennox writes, 'We might say that uniform experience over the past 300 years shows that kings of England are not decapitated. If you knew this, and were faced with the claim that King Charles I was decapitated, you might refuse to believe it because it went against the uniform experience. You would be wrong! He was beheaded. Uniformity is one thing: absolute uniformity is another.'

ii)   Similarly with the argument about the absolute consistency of experience, and Hume disallowing any exceptions. What Hume is actually saying is that for something to be a miracle it has to be an entirely unprecedented event, never before experienced, because if it had occurred before it would not, then, be a miracle. 'We may conclude,' he writes in his *Enquiry*, 'that the Christian religion not only was at first attended with miracles, but even at this day cannot be believed by any reasonable person without one'. In fact, Hume has no cause for saying that, for an event to be a miracle, it has to be unprecedented. For this reason, Lennox concludes that Hume is 'simply assuming what he wants to prove – that nature is uniform, and that no miracles have taken place!'

To move to a more contemporary view of miracles, William James seemed to be impressed by what, in the *Varieties of Religious Experience*, he termed 'miraculous conversion', and he provided several examples. The most striking of these, perhaps, was the conversion in 1842 of a French Jew, Alphonse Ratisbonne. While in Rome, instead of waiting for a friend who had to visit the church of Sant'Andrea delle Fratte, he decided to follow him and take a look at the church himself. Inside he had a life-changing vision of the Virgin Mary, a subject beyond his own religious and cultural context. James gives us Ratisbonne's own and very full account. 'In an instant . . . the whole church had vanished, I no longer saw anything . . . or more truly I saw, O my God, one thing alone. Heavens, how can I speak of it. Oh no! human words cannot attain to expressing the inexpressible . . . I was there, prostrate on the ground, bathed in tears . . .' James follows the account with this comment, 'I might multiply cases almost indefinitely, but these will suffice to show you how real, definite, and memorable an event a sudden conversion may be to him who has the experience.' Those who are already adherents of the God-hypothesis will be impressed by such accounts of miraculous conversion; the nature or cause of the experience are, however, interpreted by its detractors as delusional and auto-suggested.

The above discussion suggests that, because of nature's irregularities, we can never be absolutely sure that the laws of nature will continue to operate as they always have. Nor can we be sure that unprecedented experience of the contravention of natural laws will never happen again. In allowing that our understanding of natural law will change according to our increasing knowledge of it, and that new laws may be discovered, Hume contradicts himself. He can't hold to both the uniformity of nature and the *possibility* that natural law might change. Similarly, he contradicts his thesis that experience is also uniform. He illustrates the point with the example that we can't be absolutely sure the sun will rise tomorrow simply because it has always risen. This is, of course, an extreme and obvious example, and one that suggests miracles are, by definition, improbable, and that any event that is claimed to be miraculous would need to be backed by a form of evidence. But what is evidence for a miracle, beyond the eyewitness accounts of those observing it?

It is this lack of evidence that so troubles the atheists, who find it incomprehensible that anyone can believe in miracles. But theists have always maintained that the accounts of biblical miracles were corroborated either by the subjects themselves or by eyewitnesses. In the New Testament, for example, five thousand were fed by Jesus from five loaves and two fishes. We are not, here, concerned with proof, but with the way the accounts of the miracles record the witnesses to them. Analysts of the synoptic gospels (Matthew, Mark and Luke) agree, even allowing for editorial influence, that when a record appears in all three of them, that record is more than likely to be historically accurate. The account of the feeding of the five thousand appears in all four of the canonical Gospels.

As we have seen, in the process of adapting to the scientific age, religions (and Christianity in particular) have moved away from a literal belief in the Bible. It is possible to interpret the miracles as pictures, or stories, illustrating both the direct and indirect power of God, rather than accepting them as actual historical interventions. But Christianity itself cannot deny the miraculous, since its entire faith is hung on miracles, notably those of the virgin birth and the resurrection. (See 'Death and Survival', below.) Atheists contend that, by believing in miracles, theists themselves bring religion into disrepute and that their doing so contributes to the case against them. They concluded that miracles, understood as suspensions of natural law, belong to a former age when what people believed was determined by the authoritative teachings of the Church and a culture of superstition. For atheists, the authority of religious institutions still conditions what people believe and, even though outmoded by the scientific age, superstition continues to influence, for instance, believers in the New Age faiths.

If a miracle is an event that suspends natural laws that were put in place by God in the process of creating the universe, how, ask atheists, did God decide which laws to construct? In the lecture to the National Secular Society referred to above, Bertrand Russell asked the same question: 'Why did God issue just those natural laws and no others? If you say that he did it simply from his own good pleasure, and without any reason, you then find that there is something which is not subject to law, and so your train of natural law is interrupted. If you say, as more orthodox theologians do, that in all the laws which God issues he had a reason for giving those laws rather than others – the reason, of course, being to create the best universe, although you would never think it to look at it – if there was a reason for the laws which God gave, then God himself was subject to law, and therefore you do not get any advantage by introducing God as an intermediary.' On this argument, Hume's assertion that a miracle is a violation of the laws of nature calls into doubt the usefulness of identifying a miracle as a violation of law.

Finally, it is useful to make a distinction between the miraculous and the supernatural. Professor Lennox has made the point that, while the miraculous will always be supernatural, the supernatural will not always be miraculous. If you believe in a creator God, then the entire creation of the universe is a supernatural event; but it is not miraculous, because the whole process is held together by natural law. The paranormal, ghosts, poltergeists, spirits and spirit possession are all manifestations of the supernatural, but they are not miraculous, nor are they necessarily dependent on a belief in God. They are not miraculous since supernatural events (by definition) conform to laws above and beyond natural law; they transcend them rather than suspend them. However, the supernatural is of considerable interest to scientists, and university departments have been established to research these phenomena – notably at the universities of Edinburgh and Bristol in the UK and at the universities of Virginia and Harvard in the USA. While they do not necessarily have any direct bearing on the God-hypothesis, such phenomena are taken to be a clear indication of a dimension beyond the 'normal' or natural, and they constitute a subject for research that some atheists, as well as theists, would support, and in which they already participate.

2. Death and Survival

The fact of death, and the possibilities of surviving it offered by the various religions, are among the most sensitive issues of the God-debate.

There are two basic responses we can make to the certainty that, one day, we will die: we can accept death as something built into the structure of life which, except for forms of violent death or the instance of suicide, is – like birth – an entirely involuntary and natural event; or we can think of death, to use the stark phrase of William James, as the 'worm at the core' of human happiness. What it amounts to is the way we, unlike other animals, live with the knowledge of our mortality and how we gradually acquire this knowledge. In *Denial of Death*, Ernest Becker distinguishes between two attitudes to death. The first suggests that a fear of death is not natural; we are not born with it. Child studies have shown that the fear of death, and of other anxieties stemming from it, is something that develops gradually. When the fact of death makes itself apparent, the child either accommodates it comfortably or it becomes the source of deep anxiety, the difference depending on whether or not the earlier experiences of the child are good or bad, happy or unhappy. This suggests that the way we think and feel about death is a matter of nurture not nature. Conversely, there are those such as William James who believe the fear of death is both innate and entirely natural, a basic fear that gives rise to many other fears and anxieties. In *The Varieties of Religious Experience*, he expounds on this very clearly: 'The fact that we *can* die, that we *can* be ill at all, is what perplexes us; the fact that we now, for a moment, live and are well is irrelevant to that perplexity. We need a life not correlated with death, a health not liable to illness, a kind of good that will not perish, a good in fact that flies beyond the Goods of nature.' Whatever the joys, the happiness, the contentment and successes of the moment, these are experienced against their transitory character and our fear of death. This view holds that the anxieties it engenders are an entirely natural response. Few of us are conscious of this fear all of the time. We are so preoccupied with the business of getting on with life and making the best we can of it that the true nature of death and its implications confronts us only at specific times – when a friend or relative dies, say, or we find our own life threatened. But the truth of death, its unmitigated fact, is as universal as the fear of it. It is argued by atheists that fear of death, more than anything else, predisposes theists to a belief in God and the possibility of survival and eternal life. Such a hope, say the atheists, is merely a cushion softening the impact of death's stark reality.

For atheists, the matter is simple: beyond the biological run of life there is nothing but life's negation. We are born, we live, we die. To what extent this severe agenda generates fears and anxieties for opponents of the God-hypothesis, only they can say. Presumably, they face and come to terms with their own and other people's deaths with honest realism and accept that death is the natural and inevitable end of life. But for believers in the God-hypothesis there is more to be said. The fear of death, and the hope of surviving whatever might threaten this present life, or might merit eternal life, is addressed more by religion than by anything else. What possibilities of survival does religion offer?

Few, if any, religious traditions today teach that death itself can be avoided, since to do so would be to admit the concept of physical immortality – the possibility of being born with a body that is not subject to death. Physical immortality is not the same as eternal life, which is the expectation of surviving death in a mode of existence that does not take physical form (although there are those who believe it does) and for which death is the means or gateway.

One possibility of surviving death physically would be by means of bodily resurrection – as with that of Jesus of Nazareth, belief in which lies at the heart of the Christian faith and for the accounts of which the Gospels provide eyewitnesses. (Matthew 28, Luke 24, and John 20–21.) The resurrection of Jesus is the source of the believers' hope, either of their own physical resurrection or, differently interpreted, of surviving in another mode of being. For Christians, the resurrection of Jesus represents God's victory over death, a rite of passage that was not a part of the original blueprint of creation. Resurrection further demonstrates God's triumph over evil, which is held responsible for death's intrusion into God's plan for human life. Although these ideas are deeply ingrained and have been hugely influential in Western consciousness, the actual physical resurrection of Jesus, or of anyone as an historical event, is a difficult case to argue and one which atheists dismiss as a wish-fulfilling myth. But it is so basic to Christianity that atheists need to take into account that it is precisely this so-called 'myth' of resurrection that has received much attention from 'demythologizers' such as Bultmann, Bonhoeffer, John Robinson and others. These are committed believers in Christianity who have endeavoured to reinterpret the concept of resurrection in other than literal terms.

David Hume used resurrection as an example of a miracle (see above) and the point he argued is that, if a religion is founded on a miracle such as resurrection, its followers have a right to expect to be witnesses of further miracles if their faith is to be sustained. This expectation, he explained, is based on his argument referred to, from precedent and improbability. The resurrection and post-resurrection appearances were unprecedented for those who witnessed them; but for the general concept of miracle to be valid, Hume asserted, miracles should recur for each generation so as to be unprecedented for them, too. If the assumption is made that the universe has its origin in some form of supernatural power, then the possibility of something like resurrection falls naturally within the structure of that universe. Since most atheists reject any form of supernaturalism, they also reject the concept of resurrection.

The claim of traditional Christianity has been for a form of physical survival in what is termed a 'new' or 'uncorrupted' body that has never lived before but will continue to do so eternally. Christians argue that Jesus' execution was not the end of his life, that there was an event greater or wider than his life, one which Karl Peters, a former Professor of Religion, terms the 'Christ-event'. Those who experienced that event with Jesus found his resurrected body to be real enough, and the doubting Thomas was invited to feel the wounds Jesus sustained during his crucifixion (John 20:27) so as to allay his doubts about the physical character of the post-resurrection appearances. For many Christians, the physical resurrection of Christ is the foundation of their faith; they do not suffer with that sense of loss associated with a final death but find themselves richly fulfilled by their identity with 'the living Christ'. Put simply and unambiguously, Christians believe that Jesus' death was real but, having died, he came back to life. Except for Christian fundamentalists and the more conservative believers, the traditional concept of the survival of the body, it being raised from the grave and resuscitated, has fallen away, the implication now being that it is not the body but a non-physical essence that continues after death; what survives is the 'true' or 'real' self. The idea of such survival is not confined to Christianity; it is central to Eastern religions (see below), with other variations appealing to the mind–body–spirit movements, and to New Age religions.

Atheists do not seem to address the possibility that what may survive death is the Hebraic concept of the inherent unity of the person, a unity figured by the monotheistic concept of the unity of God that superseded the Greek duality of body and soul which has conditioned so much of Western religion and philosophy. Paul Davies, writing in *God and the New Physics*: 'Though some of these ideas [information-bearing patterns of the mind] may seem fearsome, they do hold out the hope that we can make scientific sense of immortality, for they emphasise that the essential ingredient of mind is *information*.' Davies's view of survival 'allows for the existence of disembodied minds,' of what he calls 'the enduring core of mind'. What form this might take he doesn't say, but he points out that 'most people, however, do not contemplate the survival of their entire personalities; so much of our makeup is tied to our bodily needs and capabilities'.

Reincarnation, or metempsychosis, is quite another matter. The concept of the survival of the 'real self', or *atman,* is basic to Hinduism, while Buddhism teaches that there is no real self to survive, an idea that has no part in Christianity or the other biblical religions. The Buddhist belief is that our souls, or some abiding but personal aspect of our being, have lived before in the body of another human being or animal, and that they will continue to do so after our present demise for a very long period of time, until a person gains liberation, by enlightenment, from the process of transmigration, from *samsara,* the cycle of birth, death and rebirth. This concept, also known as the transmigration of souls, was held by the Greek philosopher and mathematician Pythagoras of Samos and his followers. In the conclusion to *The Republic,* Plato tells the eschatological tale of a man called Er who, having died in battle, revives on his funeral pyre and describes his journey through the afterlife, a journey made possible by reincarnation. Although it will not convince atheists, there is something beguilingly attractive about the idea of such a continuum, of some form of personal but essential energy that has lived many lives and will continue to do so. However, the doctrine of reincarnation is not dependent on a belief in God, and it is hard to find any concept of God in Buddhism itself, for example. Reincarnation may not even be dependent on the supernatural; since what sustains life is a form of energy, its continuation in a new physical form after death may one day be explained by science.

In summary, the claim for survival of death, by whatever means and in whatever form, is generally made on the grounds that our present life is incomplete, that we all die with unfinished business and that, in terms of our potential and its realization, life in some form must continue.

3. Ethics and Morality

The issue can be stated quite simply: is the God-hypothesis a necessary basis for ethical and moral standards? Although atheists, like most people, have been influenced by the religious culture into which they were born, they hold that a belief in God, or any other form of super-natural being, is entirely unnecessary as the source of our moral values. The psychologist Carl Rogers indicated that we are born with an innate and instinctive sense of right and wrong that is developed by our environment and education. In *A Philosophy of Persons*, a section in *The Carl Rogers Reader*, he explained that, 'in choosing what course of action to take in any situation, many people rely upon guiding principles, upon a code of action laid down by some group or institution, upon the judgement of others, or upon the way they have behaved in some similar situation in the past . . . They discover, to an ever-increasing degree, that if they are open to their experience, doing what "feels" right proves to be a competent and trustworthy guide to behaviour . . . They are surprised at their own intuitive skill in finding behavioural solutions to complex and troubling human relations.' Cultural and social anthropologists such as Claude Lévi-Strauss and Margaret Mead have suggested that our innate moral sense becomes entirely socially orientated, human groups having established mores and laws that have cultivated traits of character and behavioural patterns that define a person's responsibility to the group and the group's responsibility to the person. As these communities develop into more extended societies, such standards have become fixed in tradition and enforced by law.

Whether or not the ethical and moral code is believed to be inherent, or to have originated in a theistic or polytheistic context, the ethical systems of different societies across the world show divergent standards and values. For example, while tribal Africa, Bible-belt America, Middle England or Saudi Arabia have a coherent and comprehensive system of law that covers most aspects of both the individual's and the group's existence, the basis and nature of their ethical systems are markedly different. In each of these societies there will be both absolute, inviolable principles and relative values that allow for changes or modifications of custom and law. The considerable variety of these different moral codes, and their wide-ranging, and sometimes contradicting values, make it difficult for theists to argue that there is just one divine source for them all.

One of the problems for a religion-based morality is that it presupposes that our moral judgements will be made in favour of God's goodness, his omnibenevolence. Theists have persistently pointed out that a perfectly good God would *always* act in such a way as to do the most good; in which case, God has no free will, he cannot make choices and thus cannot be described as being 'moral'. In *The Phenomenon of Religion*, Moojan Momen, a writer on the Baha'i faith, suggests that if God does exist, but is not the basis for morality and goodness, these must come from a different source.

The case for a rational, secular morality has a very long history, going back to ancient Greece and its concept of *arete,* or virtue. The sophist Protagoras challenged the idea of a fixed, determining reality by stating that man is the measure of all things. Socrates advanced the cause by regarding virtue as the rational part of the human psyche, that is the soul or mind. In our own time, the multi-cultural and multi-religious character of society provides numerous theories about the origins of our sense of right and wrong, and frequently these are conflicting. Among them, for example, are the evolutionary biologists who propose that certain patterns of behaviour are necessary for the survival of the species. That is to say, within any group, conformity to the accepted standards of behaviour is more likely to ensure the immediate well-being of the group, and in the long term, its survival. This might seem to be a self-interested, functional, utilitarian morality, reminiscent of Jeremy Bentham's Utilitarianism, that seems to offer little scope for altruism. Dawkins, however, tells us this is not the whole story. He coined the phrase 'selfish gene', to describe the idea that the greater the genetic similarity between two individuals, the more sense it makes for them to be cooperative, that is less selfish, with each other. Dawkins follows this through to suggest that, 'There are circumstances – not particularly rare – in which genes ensure their own selfish survival by influencing organisms to behave altruistically.' He goes on to outline various Darwinian 'pillars' of altruism, such as kinship, reciprocation, and the benefit for survival of acquiring a reputation for generosity and kindness. 'Throughout most of our prehistory,' Dawkins comments, 'humans lived under conditions that would have strongly favoured the evolution of altruism.' The anthropologists would agree. Nature has thus dispensed a sense of right and wrong, a concern for others which, for animals, is inborn and instinctive, and for humans inborn but made rational by education and experience, although we still retain something of our original instinctive feeling for what we ought to do. That nature endowed us with an innate sense of concern for others was an idea of interest to philosophers such as Hume and Rousseau. What most atheists are arguing for here is the concept that an innate sense of right and wrong, and the way this is brought into conformity with the group, is part of the evolutionary process that contributes to our survival. This, more general form of argument implies that, for us to know the difference between right and wrong, we have no need at all for the God-hypothesis. We are capable of doing good on our own; we are also capable of doing evil.

In one way or another, how we behave is determined by the consequences of what we do or don't do, and in Western culture these consequences have been traditionally defined by religion. Only relatively recent movements towards secularization have brought about distinctions between church, civil, criminal and common law, and between a religion-based morality and its alternatives. It might seem, therefore, that to abandon religion as the basis for morality liberates us from the consequences of what is traditionally labelled as 'sin'. Theists are concerned that, set free of religious restraint, the ensuing relative values would plunge society into anarchy. Christian apologists argue that only a moral philosophy based on God's biblical laws, set out in the Ten Commandments and the Sermon on the Mount, can provide a cohesive ethical system, and that undermining the foundation of these established values has led to an unreliable, arbitrary, subjective and voluntary code of conduct. Related to the question of restraint is the fear of punishment or the hope of reward for the way we behave. Einstein famously said that, 'If people are good only because they fear punishment and hope for reward, then we're a sorry lot indeed.' Michael Shermer, science historian and founder of the American Skeptics Society, writes in *The Science of Good and Evil,* 'If you agree that, in the absence of God, you would commit robbery, rape, and murder, you reveal yourself as an immoral person ... If, on the other hand, you admit that you would continue to be a good person even when not under divine surveillance, you have fatally undermined your claim that God is necessary for us to be good.'

Immanuel Kant, although not a secularist, worked towards his moral system on the basis of 'pure reason'. He was not interested in trying to replace the basis on which we make ordinary moral judgements, even less to develop a new moral system. He made it clear in his second *Critique* that 'no new principle is set forth ... but only a new formula'. That formula, which he called the 'categorical imperative', stated that we should 'act only on the maxim which you can at the same time will to become a universal law'. Such a maxim provides a standard, or test, by which we can judge the rightness or wrongness of our behaviour.

A formative movement in the history of moral philosophy, already referred to, was an ethical doctrine known as Utilitarianism, and its principal advocates were Jeremy Bentham and John Stuart Mill. Mill's well-known utilitarian formula is known as 'the greatest happiness principle'. In *On Liberty*, he explained that the principle 'holds that actions are right in proportion as they tend to promote happiness, wrong as they tend to promote the reverse of happiness. By happiness is intended pleasure and the absence of pain; by unhappiness, pain and the privation of pleasure.' It might seem like a manifesto for hedonism, but the ideal is 'the greatest happiness of the greatest number'.

Atheists would probably feel comfortable with moral theories of this kind since their authority is not dependent on a belief in God. More liberal theists might argue that these bases for morality are similar to St Augustine's idea, considered previously, 'Love God and do as you as like.' Both views assume the voluntary acceptance of responsibility.

The theist argument for a God-based morality calls into question the shortcomings of an atheistic, humanistic moral system, especially with regard to ethically demanding and sensitive questions such as abortion, euthanasia and capital punishment. The decisions made in any of these areas are based on moral values and, however the problem is resolved, strong arguments can be put forward for both sides. There are no scientific criteria that enable us to be sure that the decision taken is the right one; each case might have been resolved in a different, even contradictory way. In whatever manner such finely balanced decisions are made, we must hope they were both informed and as objective as possible. While knowledge informs the decision, the decision itself reaches for something beyond knowledge. That it does so is not, necessarily, an argument for a God-based morality, but it is an argument against, for example, Bertrand Russell's view, and one held by many scientists and philosophers, that 'whatever knowledge is attainable, must be attained by scientific method'. All decisions are better made when they are as fully informed as possible; science may provide us with the necessary information needed to make that decision; it can inform us of the facts, the data, the pros and cons; in the end, however, well-informed moral judgements are made without recourse to science, making their appeal to our intuition and to that inner sense of what is right.

The argument for absolute transcendent values has a long history. Plato taught that we can rightly direct our actions only when we know the absolute basis of any moral virtue. Furthermore, we can only judge the rightness or wrongness of any action when we have acquired knowledge of those absolute values. We have, Plato concluded, no real basis for living our lives in a morally correct manner unless we are dependent on the existence of an absolute Good. Aristotle was uneasy with ethical absolutes and took a different, relative view of morality. He wanted to avoid self-existing absolutes, arguing that the Idea of the

Good could never be relevant to every situation in which we find ourselves, and that therefore there are only good and bad people, good and bad actions, existing in many different contexts. Plato argued that morality stemmed from metaphysics, Aristotle that it lay in things 'as they are', in the particular and individual. In one sense, it is the difference between Idealism and Realism, absolutism and relativism, and as such the agenda was set for all future discussions on morality.

This distinction between absolute and relative, or situational ethics, is the watershed of moral philosophy; while theists and atheists may wander on either side of it and across it, in the end they are divided by it. Theists such as the philosophical theologian Paul Tillich and the philosopher of religion and aesthetics Mark Taylor have abandoned trying to prove the existence of God from metaphysical arguments. However, they still hold to the view that God can be shown to exist in the moral consciousness of the believer. For such a person, morality is of ultimate value and everything else is subordinated to it. The theist argues, for example, that neither science nor art, nor even the commitment of people to each other, are sure enough foundations for the moral life, since each of these can be put to selfish and cruel purposes. And the believer in God is faced precisely with this dilemma if called upon to take life in defence of the values held to be important. The important question is always raised: to what extent are we free to make the decisions we know we should make? That issue, the degree of our moral freedom, will be expanded upon in a later section of this chapter. In general, atheists would argue that there are no absolute or single moral truths, that morality is relative, that what might be the right thing to do in one situation could be manifestly wrong in another. Theists tend to be more conservative, insisting on objective moral truths and, even if these are not absolute, they regard such truths as emanating from a God-centred morality. In 2008, Pope Benedict XVI contributed to the debate by declaring at the World Youth Day rally in Sydney that moral relativism leads 'to moral or intellectual confusion, to a lowering of standards, to a loss of self-respect, and even to despair'. Whether they are free or conditioned, or represent some kind of balance of these opposites, theists and atheists all live with a sense of what they *ought* or *ought not* to do.

4. Aesthetics

It would be useful for the debate if those arguing against the God-hypothesis were to reconsider the relationship between aesthetics and religious belief, a subject that has been of interest to philosophers from Aristotle to the present day. Many of these philosophers, for example Kant, Schiller and Hegel, have influenced the way we evaluate art and develop taste. There are modern thinkers, such as the philosopher Richard Swinburne, the theologian Francis Schaeffer, and the writer C S Lewis, whose case for the existence of God includes the argument from the viewpoint of aesthetics – that is, the response of the mind and our emotions to beauty. This can be understood as part of the argument from design, that the order and design on our planet and throughout the universe suggest the existence of an intelligent Orderer or Designer. The argument from aesthetics is not a new one. St Augustine wrote in his *City of God*, 'Beauty can be appreciated only by the mind. This would be impossible, if this "idea" of beauty were not found in the mind of a more perfect form . . . there must be some being in which the original form resides, unchangeable, and therefore incomparable.'

Unsurprisingly, there are people who are drawn to religion for entirely aesthetic reasons. Every religion has produced high art in the form of architecture, painting, sculpture, literature and music, and these have been used to invoke the senses and feelings associated with religious experience, such as awe, wonder, love, fear and ecstasy. It is not known why some aesthetic responses produce physical effects, such as hair-raising, trembling, tears and laughter, or at what point these evolved characteristics had important consequences for our survival. In all major world religions, art has also been used to illustrate the oral teachings of religious doctrines – from the early Middle Ages, for instance, to people who did not understand the Latin of the church's Masses and rituals. Appreciation of art is not, of course, the monopoly of believers, but those who do hold to a religious belief would agree with Albert Schweitzer that 'art is one of the greatest ways of glorifying God'.

The question put by theists is whether religious art can be created without commitment to the faith that has inspired it. Clearly, not all great religious art was the work of believers. Artists of all kinds, even those of other than Christian faith, were commissioned by the Church and by individual patrons to produce work for them. One example is the Polish Jewish sculptor Sir Jacob Epstein. His bronze sculpture *St Michael's Victory over the Devil* hangs on the outside entrance wall of the Cathedral Church of St Michael at Coventry in England. Even so, in general, theists claim that great religious art can only be created out of profound religious belief, and because such art is an expression of 'truth', it could not have been created from a false premise. However, that someone who believes in God produces consummate art as an expression of that belief is not proof of God's existence, although the art itself may require response. In his book *After Progress,* the philosopher Anthony O'Hear wrote, 'Through art, particularly the great masterpieces of the past, we do have intimations of beauty, of order, of divinity even, way beyond the biological . . . in appreciating the beauty of the world . . . we are seeing the world as endowed with value and meaning . . . In responding to our experience of the world in moral and aesthetic ways, we are implying that there is something to be responded to.'

Holding passionately to any opinion or belief is inclined to produce deep feelings and emotions, and those stemming from religious belief seem particularly prone to being obsessive. We have already been concerned with religious feeling, with Rudolf Otto's 'numinous'; but here, the argument for God rests both on the feelings brought to the creation of art and the feelings derived from observing it. Science, or forms of specialist technology, may make available to the artist the means of producing his work; it can contribute to the development of new techniques and materials; but it contributes nothing to the artist's talent and to the sense of what constitutes good or bad art. John Lennox illustrated this by pointing out that science cannot tell us whether a poem is poor or a work of genius. All science can do is provide a mechanical analysis; it can tell us the number of words the poem contains, or the number of times a given word recurs, or demonstrate the frequencies of the sounds of the words when the poem is read aloud. What enables us to determine the quality of a work of art is the aesthetic sense which combines the perception of truth with the form most suitable to its expression. The American literary critic Lionel Trilling specified 'sincerity' and 'authenticity' as critical criteria, suggesting that the energy that produces a sublimely balanced and expressive working of a piece of high art lies within the artist. The creation of such art is another argument contradicting the claim that only science is concerned with reality.

The problem, for theists and atheists alike, is that nowadays aesthetics, our sense of what is beautiful, is inseparable from Romanticism – which Richard Tarnas suggested, in his *Passion of the Western Mind*, substituted the God of mysticism, even of pantheism for the God of doctrinal orthodoxy. Romanticism is a response to the world that invokes awe and wonder, melancholy and yearning; it was a reaction to the scientific revolution and its consequent materialism, and it gave a religious dimension to the concept of beauty which was so comprehensive that, rather than just being illustrative, it turned art into a channel of religious experience. An atheistic reaction to this was broadly represented by the late 19th-century Aesthetic Movement, which endeavoured to liberate art from being utilitarian, didactic or functional, and also, most importantly, to rid it of the need to serve morality or religion. The Aesthetic Movement was the impetus behind the doctrine 'art for art's sake', a phrase first coined by the French philosopher Victor Cousin. In *The Gentle Art of Making Enemies,* James McNeil Whistler wanted to distance aesthetics from the Romanticism referred to above; he insisted that 'art should be independent of all claptrap ... should stand alone ... and appeal to the artistic sense of eye and ear, without confounding this with emotions entirely foreign to it, such as devotion, pity, love, patriotism and the like'.

It seems that while the 'art for art's sake' movement resulted in work of the highest quality, something was nevertheless lost. The English philosopher Peter Williams wrote in the *Quodlibet Journal*, 'The hypothesis that God is the only sufficient condition of the objectivity and meaningfulness of aesthetic value explains (what otherwise seems inexplicable) why the flower of artistic high culture that flourished under the world-view of Christendom turned to rancour in a secular society.' This, of course, raises the question as to the meaning and purpose of art, one that is beyond the scope of this book, but it is important, for this aspect of the debate, to understand the implications of how the meaning of art has changed. In *An Intelligent Person's Guide to Modern Culture,* Roger Scruton wrote, 'If you consider the high culture of modern times, you will be struck by the theme of alienation which runs through so many of its products . . . the high culture of our society, having ceased to be a meditation on the common religion, has become instead a meditation on the lack of it.' The sense of that lack, what people feel is missing, has itself become the subject of much of the art of contemporary culture, be it fine art, film, theatre, literature, or music. The loss that modern art regrets, say the theists, is God.

They contend that God is to be seen and encountered in all great forms of art and especially, because of its abstract nature, in music. As such, art not only offered an alternative to the scientific world-view; it also provided a means of transcending this, of experiencing a different reality through what Tarnas called 'the mystical crucible of aesthetic transformation'. In terms of Western cultural history, this 'different reality' set the pattern of the 'two cultures', art (or the humanities) and science, a dualism that is still evident to the point of requiring us to make a choice about the direction our education might take. In a Journal entry made in July 1916, Wittgenstein wrote, 'Life is the World. Ethics does not treat of the world. Ethics must be a condition of the world, like logic. Ethics and Aesthetics are one.' The relationship between ethics and aesthetics has to do with values, with what we consider to be morally good and aesthetically beautiful.

Atheists respond to the beauty of high religious art, knowing that as expressions of profound religious commitment these might be revelatory, even though they regard this as illusional. Theists respond by saying that to dismiss as illusional, or intellectually unsustainable, the religious basis of aesthetics, fails to follow the evidence where it leads; it is our aesthetic experience, they argue, that contributes indispensably to giving life meaning, and that it is fatuous to conclude that these experiences are illusional. Interestingly, Peter Williams, in the *Quodlibet Journal* article referred to above, observes that secular philosophers such as Anthony O'Hear, who writes about evolution and aesthetics, and Roger Scruton, a specialist in aesthetics, recognize that aesthetics lends itself to religious treatment. In short, that in consideration of beauty they recognize the 'pull' of theism. In his *Beyond Evolution*, O'Hear, despite his secularism, writes, 'From my point of view, it is above all in aesthetic experience that we gain the fullest and most vividly lived sense that though we are creatures of Darwinian origin, our nature transcends our origin in tantalising ways.' What the aesthetic argument for God implies is that, in our response to beauty, there is not just a yearning for the beautiful but also a desire to *become* beautiful – that the ultimate form of aesthetic experience is to be 'at one' with God.

The need for aesthetic response is symptomatic of what Pascal called a 'void'. In his *Pensées,* he wrote, 'Man tries unsuccessfully to fill this void with everything that surrounds him, seeking in absent things the help he cannot find in those that are present, but all are incapable of it. This infinite abyss can be filled only with an infinite . . . object . . . God himself.' In his afterword to *The Pilgrims Regress,* C S Lewis picked up the German word *Sehnsucht* (meaning longing, yearning, craving), which he described as the 'inconsolable longing' in the human heart for 'we know not what'. The theist argument calls on this kind of perception, that our aesthetic responses emanate from our need for an experience of the ultimate; that God exists enables a world-view in which we can, more naturally, respond to and understand aesthetic reality.

5. Free Will and Determinism

The important subject of free will, and the extent to which we exercise it, has occupied both Western and Eastern philosophy throughout history and has always been earnestly debated. The concept of freedom, of our being free to direct and control our lives, takes many forms, but theologians, philosophers and psychologists have never argued that we are entirely free, some even suggesting that we are not free at all. Freedom, it has been said, is a state of mind.

The issue is whether or not we are able to choose and act freely or whether all our behaviour, for whatever reason, is conditioned and predetermined, either by the will of God, by our DNA, or by both. Atheists hold that what we take to be free choice is qualified by our genetic make-up, our nurturing environment and education, by our social status and moral commitments. These, it is held, condition us to a considerable degree and determine the kind of person we are and our disposition to think and act in a certain way. It appears, therefore, that if we do have free will, it is relative to these formative processes.

The debate is problematic for both atheists and theists, but probably more so for the latter. Scientists, especially those opposed to the God-hypothesis, argue that everything, from the movement of the planets, the behaviour of atoms and the succession of seasons to all aspects of human behaviour, is determined by natural law and the process of evolution. The scientific claim that everything is mechanistically predetermined has been shown to be simplistic by the discovery that quantum physics at atomic levels works very differently from the process described by Newtonian physics and that, for example, Heisenberg's 'uncertainty principle' places a limit on what we can know of the path of particles. Citing

Heisenberg, Paul Davies writes in *God and the New Physics*, 'The most important argument, however, against complete predictability is the quantum factor. According to the basic principles of the quantum theory, nature is inherently unpredictable ... In the microworld, events occur that have no well-defined cause.'

Evolutionary biologists who propose that everything we do is inevitable because of the nature of our DNA are faced with the problem of endless deviations and aberrations in human behaviour. These exceptions are so numerous and take so many different forms that inevitability seems too strong a word to describe our behaviour. So unlimited are our behavioural variations that the margin between free will and determinism becomes blurred to the point of being indistinguishable, making it very difficult to decide if we act out of our own volition or because we are conditioned to do so. Paul Davies says of determinism that 'every decision – every whim – is determined in advance. If that is so, however free you may feel to choose tea or coffee, in reality your choice was destined from the moment you were born – even before. In a fully deterministic universe *everything* is determined from the instant of the creation. Does this make us less free? ... As soon as God is injected into the picture we bring down on ourselves a deluge of puzzles.' If God is omnipotent, then he can choose to do anything he wants; our own power is very limited: we can decide between tea and coffee only so long as the supplies last; then, if we are thirsty, we are 'forced' to another decision when we want a drink.

Biblical predestination is a theological doctrine developed by John Calvin, the French theologian and Protestant reformer. The doctrine became known as 'Calvinism'. Put briefly, it teaches that everything, all events and all human destiny, has been willed by God, even to the point that God 'predetermined' those destined to be damned and those chosen for salvation (Romans 8:29–30). Religious adherents who hold to the doctrine of predestination are faced with a concept of a God who has constructed a mechanistic universe, one that determines both the nature and purpose of life. It is a doctrine of creation that questions both our freedom to make choices and our responsibility for the choices we make. We might well ask, what is the point of all this, what value is there in being human, if the whole universe and all of life is little more than God's plaything, an emanation of his own will as an end in itself? Even though the disciple might argue that the surrender of one's will to God is freely volunteered, it amounts to the same 'no-will' situation, since everything we think and do is fixed by the divine will. To this we must add that, even if we make decisions out of a will surrendered to God, is it this same God that has built into creation the suffering and misery caused by many of the decisions we do seem to make?

The doctrine, however, even within Calvinism, poses some important questions. For example, does God make a predetermining decision based on his own will or because, being omniscient, he already knows what will happen? Are his decisions made with regard to general events and large groups of people, or do they concern particular events and particular people? Is God himself free, or is he limited by conditions outside of his own will? Because God is taken to be all-knowing and all-powerful, the implication is that, if we have free choice, it is because he is also self-limiting and that he qualifies his omnipotence so as to allow us our sense of freedom. In section 3 above, which discussed ethics and morality, it was noted that if God is all good, omnibenevolent, then he can choose only to do good, that his own goodness makes it impossible for him to choose otherwise, since in any given situation he must do the 'right thing'.

The catechism of the Roman Catholic Church has a neat response to the conflict that exists in Calvinism between predestination and human free will: 'To God, all moments of time are present in their immediacy. When therefore he establishes his eternal plan of "predestination", he includes in it each person's free response to his grace.' The concept of grace, as a response to the issue of free will and determinism, also concerned St Augustine, who taught that humans were endowed with free will by God's grace and, since they act freely, he argues that in respect of the presence of evil in a world created by a beneficent God, it is they and not God who are responsible for evil. Aquinas bases his case for free will on the intellect, the God-given faculty that enables us to consider, reflect, and reconsider the reasons for any course of action. The will is free, but subject to the intellect that makes or revises its judgements. Aquinas also argues that because God is outside time, the imposition of his will does not necessarily imply predestination. It is a point taken up by C S Lewis in his book *Mere Christianity*: 'But suppose God is outside and above the Time-line. In that case, what we call "tomorrow" is visible to him in just the same way as what we call today. All the days are "Now" for Him. He does not remember you doing things yesterday, He simply sees you doing them: because, though you have lost yesterday, He has not. He does not "foresee"you doing things tomorrow, He simply sees you doing them: because, though tomorrow is not yet there for you, it is for Him. You never supposed that your actions at this moment were any less free because God knows what you are doing.'

Wittgenstein thought that the enigma of free will was a 'pseudo-problem', a term coined by Moritz Schlick, the founding father of logical positivism. The problem is 'pseudo' because Wittgenstein believed it was among those kinds of problems (like the existence of God) that cannot be solved, but, to use Wittgenstein's word, only 'dissolved' by careful analysis of the language used. He questions the way we use the terms 'free will' and 'determinism' because, in making them mutually exclusive, we miss the fact that there are various gradations of usage between them. 'Willing,' he says in *Philosophical Investigations*, 'if it is not to be a sort of wishing, must be the action itself. It cannot be allowed to stop anywhere short of the action.' Our will, whether it is free or otherwise, is only realized as *our* will when it is translated into the process that brings about the purpose that is willed. The question that lurks behind this is whether there are times when God's will remains an unfulfilled wish because people hold back the cooperation necessary for fulfilling it. Are we in fact free to exercise our will, because in Eden, human disobedience set the precedent of frustrating the will of God?

As with other issues in this debate, the question of whether we have even some degree of free will cannot be empirically demonstrated. The philosophical view of this subject is clouded by its psychological implications; we do not like the idea of being wholly conditioned organisms, we love the *idea* of being free and the concept of freedom is written large into Western and Eastern philosophy; it is lauded in all cultures, even as it is enshrined in national constitutions, and wars have been fought in its defence.

The idea of free will is related to the extent to which we have moral responsibility. Given that we know enough about our behavioural patterns and the motives behind them, biology and psychology have combined to suggest that all human action can be explained causally, in which case our moral choices are not entirely free but conditioned. The question, relevant to both theists and atheists, focuses on this root issue of free will and moral responsibility. John Martin Fischer, a philosopher with a special interest in free will and moral responsibility, argues that 'causal determination rules out moral responsibility. Given that you are not morally responsible for the past, and you are not morally responsible for the laws of nature, and assuming the principle of transfer of blamelessness, causal determinism seems to rule out moral responsibility.' Theists, in whatever way they reconcile the problem of determinism, argue that morality has its roots in religion, that conscience is God-given, and that God is the sufficient, wholly determining cause of everything that happens. The American philosopher Michael J Murray argues that a good God would choose to make his existence and character less than certain for human beings, for the sake of their freedom. It is 'good' that human beings freely choose to act in obedience to his will. Any form of determinism would mean that they acted out of necessity rather than freedom.

The Buddhist response to this enigma is relieved of theistic implications. It understands freedom, as noted previously, in terms of liberation from *samsara*, the cycle of birth, death and rebirth, a liberation that can be realized through a meditation practice that leads to enlightenment. Christian believers in the God-hypothesis would say that only faith in God can set us free, and in so doing they are referring to a God that is very different from the God of the predestinationists. What Christians are set free from is sin, and this liberation is achieved through faith in Jesus Christ, whose death, on the pattern of Old Testament sacrifice, 'paid' the price necessary for human transgression of God's law. This theological concept of freedom says very little about the extent to which our choices are freely made. Hidden within this theology, moreover, is another problem theists must face. If freedom, in ultimate terms, is the prize of faith, what of those who are not recipients of the gift of faith? Are they unfree and 'destined' to the consequences of unbelief, whatever these may be?

Ethically, if we are not free to do something, then we have no duty to do it. As H J Paton put it, 'I ought, implies I can,' but the issue is rarely as simple as this. There are so many situations in which we do not have the freedom to act; we know we 'ought' to do something but for various reasons such as distance, physical inability or a limited budget, we find there is nothing we can do. Since we could not live fully and creatively if we knew that everything we do is conditioned, even determined, our sense of freedom may be psychologically necessary – we assume we are free, we all live *as though* we are free to act within parameters of the moral principles of our society. We have no sense that our likes and dislikes, or our wants or impulses, are determined. And this sense of freedom is not confined to our moral or aesthetic values and choices, it applies also to our choice of work and profession. Yet even in this context we are influenced by our interests, our knowledge and skills and, more poignantly, by the job-market. Unemployment, for example, reduces our choice to the necessity of accepting whatever work is available. The assumption of freedom sets the ambiance of our lives, and it is an assumption made by both theists and atheists.

This sub-debate between freedom and determinism is a key issue for the God-debate because it raises the question of the nature of faith in relation to the extent of our freedom. Atheists do not take sufficiently into account that faith, as Eagleton pointed out in *Reason, Faith and Revolution,* 'is not in the first place a matter of choice. It is more common to find oneself believing something than to make a conscious decision to do so . . . This is not, needless to say, a matter of determinism – it is not primarily a question of the will . . . As long as it exists, however, belief will continue to be falsely linked to so-called acts of will, in a voluntaristic misunderstanding of how we come by our convictions.'

6. Love

Traditionally, Christianity, perhaps more than any other major religion, is identified as a religion of love, that is, love of various kinds, which is made explicit in the writings of the New Testament. Pointing to a few examples, Paul's famous paean to love in 1 Corinthians 13 pleads for love as the one indispensable quality for a meaningful life: 'So faith, hope, and love abide, these three; but the greatest of these is love.' In his first letter, John pleads, 'Let us love one another; for love is of God, and he who loves is born of God and knows God. He who does not love does not know God; for God is love' (1 John 4:8). Christians understand that, on the strength of Jesus' example, there is no greater demonstration of love than forfeiting your life for your friends, a concept raised to a new level when Jesus also gave up his life for his enemies. 'God *is* love,' John asserts, an identity which allows the logical inversion, 'love is God', a definition of God that, for the purposes of the God-debate, atheists should perhaps give thought to.

The history of Christianity, at least with regard to its inextricable involvement in politics and mission, is not a shining demonstration of its creed of love. Nevertheless, it is likely that its concept of love has given the religion its widespread appeal. But no religion could claim a monopoly of love, a point vehemently argued by those opposed to the God-hypothesis. Regardless of the assertions made by New Testament writers, the love we have for other people may be genuine, sincere and lasting without it being sourced in religious belief. To say love can be irrational, that our capacity to forgive even the most extreme offence perpetrated against ourselves or others is an expression of love, and that our sense of wonder at the world about us engenders a feeling of loving gratitude for life itself, is not an argument for the existence of God. To believe 'God is love' is a statement of faith, but based on an anthropomorphism of emotions or feelings and a quality of relationship that everyone understands and has in common. Everyone loves, and most will know what love is for them, even though it may be ineffable.

While they may concede that religion played its part in promoting the cause of love, atheists remain suspicious of the role love plays in the upbringing and education of children by parents with committed religious beliefs. Dawkins points out that one major feature of religion is 'intense love focused on God'. He argues that love in a religious context has something of the same quality as romantic love and that it might merely be a 'by-product of the irrationality mechanisms that were originally built into the brain by selection, for falling in love'. Throughout history there has been a clear conjunction between religion and love, or more specifically between love and how a relationship with God has been described. The ecstatic language and imagery of love has always been employed by saints and mystics, as well as ordinary people, to describe the intensity of their relationship with God. Many examples are to be found, in the Psalms, the Song of Solomon and throughout religious literature.

Dawkins further argues that another unpalatable consequence of the conjunction between love and religion is the ethic of monogamy, the commitment to one partner. He interprets this as an image of the exclusive commitment Christianity and other religions require to be given to the one God. The biological anthropologist Helen Fisher, in her book *Why We Love*, discusses the irrationality of romantic love and the nature of monogamous commitment to one partner. She suggests that polyamory, the practice of having more than one intimate relationship at the same time with the knowledge and consent of all involved, is more rational, and in so doing she questions the tradition of the exclusiveness we give and expect to be given by a partner. In posing the thought-provoking question referred to above – could irrational religion stem from the same mechanisms that are concerned with romantic love? – Dawkins finds a relationship between the irrationality of this kind of love and the exclusive commitment it seems to require, and the unreasonableness of faith in a God who demands the same kind of exclusive commitment. Interestingly, there are several references to God being jealous: for example Exodus 34:14, 'for you shall worship no other god, for the Lord, whose name is Jealous, is a jealous God.'

Theists argue that faith is a particular form of love, and Kierkegaard, despite his religious scepticism, conceded in *Sickness unto Death* that 'a believer, after all, is someone in love'. In this context, Terry Eagleton pointed out that both Augustine and Aquinas taught that 'love is the precondition of truth' and, echoing Paul, that it is the source of all other virtues. Eagleton writes, 'Love is the ultimate form of soberly disenchanted realism, which is why it is the twin of truth,' and why, inasmuch as it has this relationship with truth, it is at best neither romantic nor irrational.

Any distinction that might be made between the view of love held by theist and atheist has to do with a sense of the absolute. For the rationalist atheist, love is one of life's basic virtues or qualities, its purpose being to define, secure and sustain inter-human relationships without any recourse to a God-hypothesis. Conversely, the theists view love as *agape,* which in its highest and purest form also secures and sustains our relationships, but, as Paul Tillich suggested, only by 'adapting itself to every concrete situation . . . to the basic absolute of all, being itself'. Intriguingly, Tillich understood his frequently used image of God as the 'ground of being' to be characterized by 'the feminine element of being', giving to his notion of love the aspect of motherhood, of being coming into life, and of nurturing that life. Although, in Western philosophy, Tillich was innovative in introducing this feminine aspect to a concept of God that is traditionally masculine, atheists are not likely to be persuaded by it. But his concept of love as a power for renewal and reunification should resonate with them.

Atheists, of course, argue that to love God is to love a delusion, since the object of that love is not demonstrable. Would they say the same of a love of self, a concept no more demonstrable than the soul or God? The love of self is considered by philosophers and psychologists to be of equal importance to our well-being as the love of others. Love of oneself can become narcissism or an extreme form of egoism, but it is held in balance by our love of others which, in a religious context, is a measure of a person's spirituality, but which also, in a secular or humanist context, is the measure of a person's unconditional 'selflessness'. The point here is that, whether or not love is sourced metaphysically, our love of others is centred and focused on something essentially practical, on Tillich's 'concrete situation' referred to above. Sustaining responsibility to the object of love is more to do with an act of the will than with an emotion or feeling. It is commitment, and it is in making this commitment to others that theists claim is one way to find God, their 'Eternal Thou', the delusion to which atheists object.

This section on Love (which, like all the other subjects in this chapter, is one that recurs in the God-debate) opened with a reference to Christianity being a religion that carries love at its centre. That was qualified by pointing out that Christian history, and thus the greater part of 2,000 years of Western history, does not demonstrate that love has been the driving motive or influence. This is not to deny the transforming power of love, compassion and care that bettered the lives of millions eventually to produce the 'caring society'. Love, however, is only one of the energies resulting in social reform, others being the drive for equality, justice, and the means of production to meet people's material needs – as, for example, was to be seen in Marx and Engels's materialist interpretation of history and the radical reforms resulting from their social theories.

Following this through, a distinction has to be made between private and public love, or what Eagleton terms 'political love'. He makes the point that 'for the liberal humanist legacy to which Ditchkins [Dawkins/Hitchens] is indebted, love can really be understood only in personal terms ... The concept of political love ... would make little sense to Ditchkins. Yet something like this is the ethical basis for socialism.' (Eagleton goes so far as to want love to be a political principle, one that will help achieve his own goal, the rejuvenation of the socialist Left.) The problem for both parties is that the word 'love', like the word 'God', has been debased in popular usage. Love is everywhere peddled by the media as being, to use Eagleton's categories, either 'erotic, romantic, or domestic'. The legacy of political love, or what can be thought of as social ethics, has its origin in religion, both in the West and the East. Theists will continue to hold to its religious origins, that love is inspired and gifted by God, while atheists will continue to understand love as an entirely humanistic quality. If this is true, then the atheist is left with some searching questions. Persuaded as they are by the processes of Darwinian evolution, did love (and the behaviours associated with it) derive from genetic mutation? What environmental pressures accompanied this mutation and in what way did this ensure survival?

7. Secularism

The arguments on which the debate about the God-hypothesis are based not only represent beliefs, they also imply purpose. Given that atheists and theists have radically different world-views, what do they want to achieve for themselves as individuals, for their groups and for society as a whole? What kind of a world do they envisage? What are they arguing *for*, rather than against? It is clear from the history of the past 2,000 years that, ideally, the biblical religions have worked for society to become a theocracy, the Kingdom of God on Earth, a form of government in which the representatives of their respective religions rule in the name of God. Judaism, based on the Old Testament model of a Jewish commonwealth, is not evangelical; it has no mandate to make the world Jewish, and the long quest for a Jewish state, and its establishment in 1948, was driven by the historical concept of a God-given 'promised land', where Jews could live freely and independently. Christianity and Islam, however, want the entire world for their respective religions, their founders mandating followers to convert people and to establish, through their representatives, the governance of God. Both Jesus and Muhammad exhort their followers to convert as many people as possible and, by so doing, effect the rule of God on Earth. The 'command' to evangelize appears in many places in their respective scriptures. The Christian's mandate is given by Jesus in, for example, Mark 16:15. The Islamic mandate is implied by the concept of *jihad,* which *The Oxford Dictionary of Islam* defines as 'a religious war with those who are unbelievers in the mission of Muhammad . . . enjoined for the purposes of advancing Islam.' (See also Surah 47:4.)

Those atheists actively contributing to the God-debate, while not mandated to evangelize, press their case in every way possible, hoping to persuade people to abandon the God-hypothesis, believing that their world-view and what they want for society is 'best', since it is founded on scientific rationalism rather than myth and delusion. Thus, the argument for atheism is an argument for radical secularism, and atheists look for a thorough-going, aggressive secularism that will combat two millennia of militant religion.

The term 'secularism' was coined by the English secularist George Jacob Holyoake in his 1896 publication *English Secularism*, in which he defined secularism as 'a code of duty pertaining to this life, founded on consider-ations purely human, and intended mainly for those who find theology indefinite or inadequate, unreliable or unbelievable. Its essential principles are three. The improvement of this life by material means. That science is the available Providence of man. That it is good to do good. Whether there be other good or not, the good of the present life is good, and it is good to seek that good.' At a conference on *The Meaning of the Secular*, held in 1959 at the Ecumenical Institute at Bosey, near Geneva, the process of secularization was defined as 'the withdrawal of areas of thought and life from religious – and finally also from metaphysical – control, and the attempt to understand and live in these areas in the terms which they alone offer'. The principle of breaking free from metaphysical control, from all religious beliefs, influences and authorities, reads like an atheist's manifesto. The terms 'secular', 'secularism' and 'secularization' describe the character of the society and culture for which atheists reach.

Secular is the antonym of sacred, and it is habitually used to distinguish between those areas of life that, having been under some form of religious authority, have achieved a degree of independence from it. One of the subjects the New Atheists argue for strongly is the secularization of education. Religious education is thought to be subversive, and atheists question the validity of schools run by churches, mosques or synagogues and the principle of state support for such schools. (See Richard Dawkins, *The God Delusion*, pp. 311–44.) Their argument is for religion to be withdrawn from the curriculum of state schools, as it has been, for example, in France.

A truly secular society, in officially abandoning the God-hypothesis, would legislate for the separation of church and state and the severing of religious links between the government and the previously adopted state religion, as exemplified by the Church of England. The right of bishops and other religious leaders to sit in the UK's House of Lords would be withdrawn, and the sovereign would no longer be the titular head of the Church. In England in the 17th and 18th centuries, religious test-clauses were instituted to exclude anyone not a member of the Church of England from holding government office – for example, Roman Catholics and non-conforming Protestants – and these criteria were carried to the colonies. In the USA, the process of secularization influenced the writing of the American constitution which states that 'no religious test shall ever be required as a qualification to any office or public trust under America'.

Similarly, all ethical and moral matters should be free of religious control. Thus, for instance, whether or not a person uses contraceptives should not be determined on religious principles by a religious authority, nor should religious belief and principle condition the criteria governing the censorship of the press, literature and other arts, or the teaching of science with regard to the theory of evolution. At the outset of the 21st century, the secularization of society is still in transition, and in the present cultural climate of both British and American politics, it seems unlikely that anyone running for high office would succeed if they declared themselves to be an atheist.

The process of secularization is not new, and the distinction between the sacred and the secular has always existed, the former carried through cultural history by established religions, the latter by dissent and legislation. While atheists want to secularize society by eliminating everything related to religion and the sacred, Christianity has always acknowledged its coexistence with the secular. Jesus made clear the distinction between a sacred and secular authority when he was asked if it was right to pay the taxes imposed by Caesar. He replied, 'Render therefore to Caesar the things which are Caesar's, and to God the things that are God's' (Matthew 22:21).

Although an aspect of the secular, the profane is not synonymous with it, since the latter carries a pejorative implication inasmuch as the profane can be irreverent, disrespectful, blasphemous or obscene. It is, therefore, necessary to make a distinction between the profane and the secular, since while the profane will always be secular, it is clear that secularism does not always amount to profanity.

Since few societies are wholly secular, even if they are declared to be so, the 'secular' is a sub-culture, a movement or state of affairs that, in itself, is amoral. Several references have been made to the movements within religions to meet the challenge of science and secularism, such as the movement to demythologize religious texts. To extrapolate biblical myths, for example, from both the Old and New Testaments is itself a secularizing process which has its sharpest expression in Bonhoeffer's phrase 'secular religion'. In a letter to Eberhard Bethage, written in April 1944, a year before he was hanged by the Nazis, Bonhoeffer wrote, 'What is bothering me incessantly is the question what Christianity really is, or indeed who Christ really is, for us today. The time when people could be told everything by means of words, whether theological or pious, is over, and so is the time of inwardness and conscience – and that means the time of religion in general. We are moving toward a completely religionless time; people as they are now simply cannot be religious any more. Even those who honestly describe themselves as "religious" do not in the least act up to it, and so they presumably mean something quite different by "religious".'

Theists have responded to the process of secularization by proposing such a 'secular religion', which may seem like a contradiction in terms but which is, however, a radical reappraisal of the meaning and function of myth in religious literature and history. Its purpose was to show that the central myths of biblical religion, such as creation, the virgin birth and resurrection of Jesus, were not essential to a faith in God because they carried a spiritual rather than a literal, historically based message.

The consequences of this movement ran far deeper than the mere debunking of mythology. It softened the hard edges of traditional dualisms such as the sacred and secular, spirit and flesh, good and evil, and thereby the polarities represented by theism and atheism. It gave the opportunity for creative dialogue between them to which the best aspects of this debate are witness.

Bruce Ledewitz is Professor of Law at Duquesne University, in Pittsburgh, USA. In his article 'The Future of God and Secularism', in the journal *Tikkun* (April/May 2010), he raises the question as to what kind of secularism will develop in the future. The New Atheists, he argues, represent a secularism that identifies God in the usual received tradition of an all-powerful, all-knowing being who demands submission. If this is going to be the on-going secularism, then that image of God will also persist. The point is that the New Atheists' mind-set preserves this outmoded concept of God, of the traditional biblical monotheistic creator, omniscient, omnipresent and so on. They have not responded to the concept of God developed by the demythologizing 'New Theologians', nor to the philosophers and philosophical theologians who have radically recast the concept of God. Ledewitz suggests that there will be a new kind of secularism that will accommodate a new concept of God. This movement he dubs, somewhat awkwardly, the 'new new secularism'. It defends ideas traditionally associated with religion but which are now the common property of people who do not owe allegiance to any particular religious tradition, yet nevertheless hold to 'the objectivity of values and the reality of mystical experience . . . and of God, the creativity at the heart of the universe'. The evolving new secularism suggests a God that is not captive to supernaturalism, and as such will be a 'God of harmony rather than division . . . a future not of holy war, but of holy community'.

In conclusion, it is important to reiterate what was stated at the beginning of this chapter, that its purpose was to heighten some specific and strongly contested issues that form a crucial part of the more general debate. Apart from the question of miracles, which assumes the existence of a God who intervenes in human affairs in such a way as to 'bend' the laws of nature, the other subjects are all constantly before us, either formally – in debate, the media or more specialist journals – or informally as we discuss these issues with friends. One way or another, everyone has their own view about life after death, even about life before birth; most endeavour to live their lives according to some common code of 'decency', while debating the 'big issues' such as capital punishment, abortion, child abuse, and the currently hot issue of personal privacy. So far as the arts are concerned each of us knows what we like; we have our own aesthetic sense and criteria for judging something as average, good or outstanding, and in that process we live as though we are free and we believe our decisions are freely made. Everyone knows something about love, the giving and receiving of it, and of its romantic abuse and misrepresentation in the popular press and the arts, and some will know of love through the tragedy of being deprived of it. Perhaps our awareness of the secular and the process of secularization is less acute; it is an issue that stands in the wings, only to take centre stage when the churches and other religious institutions intervene in the proceedings of politics and justice. To what extent any of these central issues is relevantly allied to a belief in the existence of God is a question we each have to decide for ourselves.

While this chapter has highlighted some of the subjects that most clearly divide theists and atheists, the following chapter will consider the God-debate from another point of view entirely. It will re-present the arguments in such a way as to suggest the possibility of genuine dialogue between views that appear to be irreconcilably opposed.

Chapter Eight

God and a Theory of Everything

AMONG THE NEW SCIENTISTS, whether atheists or theists, are those engaged in a search for a 'theory of everything', a formula, or a series of formulas, that would explain the origin and nature of the entire cosmos. The quest for such a theory and what this entails, is not taken up, as such, in the current debate about the God-hypothesis, but it runs below the surface. Both parties are concerned to answer basic questions such as 'Who am I?', 'Why am I here?', 'How did life and the universe originate?', and both parties believe the answers, thus far given, represent the truth 'as they see it'.

In believing in God theists presume the truth they represent to be absolute, that is, while they don't claim to know or understand everything, they do claim that because God exists, that one fact is the foundation of all knowledge; if a theory of everything was to emerge, God's existence as a unifying principle or energy, would be indispensable to it. In denying the validity of the God-hypothesis, the atheists' riposte is that the truth theists hold claim to is, in Dawkins's term, a 'delusion', and thus has no contribution to make to a unifying theory of everything.

The purpose here is to set aside discussion of the specific subjects around which the arguments revolve and to look at the broader context in which the debate is being engaged. The controversy is so important and so riven by strongly held views, that some effort must be made to see if there is any possibility of constructive dialogue between the opposing views. In so doing, it may possible that the debate which, in principle, is between the seemingly irreconcilable dualism of science and religion, may be cast in different terms. This chapter is not, therefore, about the hard-edged disputes between New Atheism and the religious establishment with its received, conventional concepts, but about other, more open-minded aspects of the debate. Not all debates are about issues that can be resolved by the use of objective proofs; they are not always concerned to establish whether a concept is right or wrong over against another concept, but about how different perceptions might be shared so as to arrive at a greater, broader truth than either view can represent alone.

The scientists' search for a theory of everything has become something like the quest for the missing-link – the scientists' grail. Writing in *Scientific American* (October 2010) Stephen Hawking said, 'the traditional expectation of a single theory of nature may be untenable, and that to describe the universe we must employ different theories in different situations'. The point of looking for a 'single theory of nature' is to come to a rational conclusion about the origin and nature of the world that can be reduced to a manageable yet comprehensive form. The problem with this is that the terms of reference and methods of enquiry may limit its outcome. That is, any possible theory sought, for example, in terms of mathematics and particle physics, would be restricted to the knowledge accessible only to those disciplines. A further problem, suggested by Paul Davies in *The Mind of God*, is that a theory of everything, whatever form it takes, has by definition to be unique and, 'if that were so, there could only be one unified system of physics, with its various laws fixed by logical necessity. Taking this line of argument to its extreme, scientists needn't bother with observation or experiment. Science would no longer be an empirical matter but a branch of deductive logic with the laws of nature acquiring the status of mathematical theorems, and the properties of the world deducible by the application of reason alone.'

The scientist's search for a theory of everything, whether pursued by theists such as the theoretical physicist John Polkinghorne, or atheists like Richard Dawkins, has something about it that is akin to religious fervour. The goal is to know and understand everything in existence and to arrive at a formulaic account of the universe, not in an abstract sense, but drawn from an empirical observation of the world using the tools available to science, for example, mathematics and quantum theory. It is thought that this 'ultimate' knowledge may be represented by a group of interconnected formulas and equations that will combine the formation of space and time with quantum and particle physics. Such a formula is currently termed string-theory, or M-theory which, it is thought, may form a network of theories. No one, says Hawking, seems to know what the 'M' represents, 'master', 'miracle', or 'mystery', but if such a theory can be found, it will amount to what he famously referred to as, 'the mind of God'.

The theist's equivalent of such a formula is not the search for a theory of any kind, but for an ultimate experience (which is understood differently by various religions), an experience that is probably best described as 'mystical'. For those whose lives are based on the God-hypothesis such an experience is a conscious union with the 'the mind of God'. For some, as noted in Chapter 5, this is a quiet, ever-present certainty, for others, it takes the form of a consuming mystical absorption, while perhaps for most, the experience is just a passing glimpse of a spiritual potential. For non-theistic religions, such as Buddhism, it is an experience that, while rooted in consciousness, transcends consciousness; it moves beyond the finite possibilities of concept, not as an intellectual construct, but as a perception and thus an experience of an alternative reality. Both atheists and theists are actually reaching for the omniscience that has traditionally been ascribed to God, the one asserting that God is superfluous in this quest, that the concept is simply not needed, while the other regards the existence of God as the indispensable foundation of their world-view.

The argument has been polarized by focusing on the issue of God's existence without due thought to the broader context in which it is debated. The one side confines itself to scientific enquiry and terms of reference, the other to theology and religious doctrine. In fact the question of God's existence cannot be answered without also asking the secondary but essential question, what does it mean to be a human being? Martin Buber asked, 'What is Man?' and responses to this, from philosophers, sociologists, anthropologists, psychologists and others, have never been entirely satisfactory because each point of view has reduced what it means to be a human being to the terms of their own discipline. No one discipline can provide a comprehensive answer, and even if a satisfactory composite answer could be given, it would only be a small contribution towards an experience or theory of everything.

Both the theists' and atheists' quest may be driven by more than curiosity and the urge for knowledge; it may also be a way of testing, or questioning, the limits biology has set on the capacity of the human intellect, and on the span of human lifetime. We are all finite, limited and temporary and, as discussed in the previous chapter, human beings have to live with the knowledge of their mortality. There is something wish-fulfilling in that, knowing we will die, we are taken with the tantalizing idea of survival, that in having finite minds we assume we can know everything, that having thoroughly mapped our own planet we now contemplate the exploration of our universe. In the shadows cast by anxieties about our mortality, there is also the question of the survival of the human race, which some believe may be threatened by the ecological problems facing the planet. Built into this quest for a theory of everything is the possibility of finding solutions to the physical problems of our continued existence; it is held by scientists that a complete knowledge of how the universe was put together, and of what sustains it, will provide the key for protecting planet Earth from the problems threatening it. Furthermore, a theory of everything would necessarily include definitive knowledge of whether this planet is unique with regard to the life it sustains, or if extra-terrestrial life does exist, either in its simplest form or as another highly intelligent animal that is unlikely to be of the human species.

As the preceding chapters have shown, there is a virulent culture of mutual suspicion between theists and atheists; it is possible that if the debate continues on its present terms, rather than achieving any meaningful dialogue, the antithesis will be heightened. Theists regard the scientific world-view as a reduction of everything to the material and mechanistic, and find it incomprehensible that atheists who are scientists are incapable of taking a broader view. In general, atheists are suspicious of religion because metaphysics is a subject better suited to mythology and the philosophy of religions than to advancing an objective and complete knowledge of our world. For atheists to allow that theists could make a contribution to a theory of everything would compromise their essential empiricism. Theists, for their part, consider that scientific principles disallow the inclusion in such a theory of a full understanding of ethics, morality, and aesthetics, or the kinds of experiences generated by introspection, intuition and feelings. More importantly, the scientist's theory would not be able to respond to the basic questions referred to above, 'Who am I?', 'Where am I going?', 'What am I here for?' Theists regard many aspects of our conscious experience, indeed, consciousness itself, as something of a mystery, and argue that psychology and philosophy have contributed more to an understanding of consciousness than has science.

From either point of view, the quest for a theory or experience of everything, raises certain questions:

i) Because both are concerned with ultimate, or absolute knowledge, is there any sense in which they are talking about, or looking for, the same thing?

ii) Is there any possibility of creative dialogue between them?

These questions cannot be asked of either biblical or scientific fundamentalists, both of whom lay claim to truths that represent irreconcilable differences. The questions are only relevant for the more open-minded debaters, those genuinely interested in dialogue. Because they recognize that each draw on different forms of knowledge and perception, it might be agreed that any theory of everything would necessarily include both scientific and religious insights. The psychiatrist Wilhelm Reich wrote, 'I know that what you call "God" really exists, but not in the form you think; God is primal cosmic energy, the love in your body, your integrity, and your perception of the nature in you and outside of you.' The geneticist and evolutionary biologist J B S Haldane said, 'the wise man regulates his conduct by the theories both of religion and science'. To achieve this kind of open-minded balance in the debate would allow creative dialogue, but to do so seems impossibly ambitious.

It has yet to be seen how the insights of philosophy, religion and science might combine in discovering the one complete theory that is a genuinely complementary melding of subjective experience and objective, empirically validated knowledge. In trying to put together an over-view of this synthesis, it is necessary to set aside the uncompromising and irreconcilable arguments that have occupied the previous chapters, and consider the ideas of the more creative thinking philosophers and scientists. It might seem that the debate between theists and atheists is between two clearly defined opponents, but they are not to be understood as two armies facing each other, dis-tinguished by their uniforms and banners and committed to winning the battle. Proponents of both views are found within every discipline, thus atheist scientists pit their arguments against scientists who believe in the existence of God, similarly with philosophers. What follows is a discussion about why, in their quest for a complete system or theory, some philosophers and scientists are theists while others are atheists.

1. The Philosophers

It is the mark of great philosophy that it has contributed to changing our existence and, at best, the process of change is brought about by balanced philosophical discourse, by synthesis rather than antithesis.

The arguments represented by the God-debate have always been engaged by philosophers. Those philosophers who have developed their systems on the basis of theism, include Anselm, Augustine of Hippo, Descartes, Hegel, Hume, Kierkegaard, Maimonides, Shankara, Spinoza, Swedenborg and Tillich. Atheist philosophers include Anaxagoras, A J Ayer, Democritus, Epicurus, Feuerbach, Lenin, Marcuse, Nietzsche, Russell, the Marquis de Sade and Schopenhauer. Regardless of the premise from which they started, many philosophers, such as Aristotle, Plato, Hegel and Descartes, Russell and Whitehead, have tried to develop a complete system, a structure of thought that enabled them to comprehend and represent our existence in all its aspects. Descartes and Russell, for example, illustrate the theist/atheist divide, even though both constructed their systems on the basis of reason.

Descartes, starting with his familiar 'I think, therefore, I am,' developed a complete philosophy of knowledge (epistemology) that included a proof of the existence of God based on a version of the ontological argument, that is, on an argument from 'being' itself. Descartes' argument, as we have seen in Chapter 3, employs intuition, something he understood as clear and distinct perception. He uses a concept of truth he had established in the *Fifth Meditation*, namely that whatever is clearly and distinctly perceived to be contained in the idea of something, is true of that thing. He wrote, 'Certainly, the idea of God, or a supremely perfect being, is one that I find within me just as surely as the idea of any shape or number. And my understanding that it belongs to his nature that he always exists, is no less clear and distinct than is the case when I prove of any shape or number that some property belongs to its nature.'

In contrast, Russell constructed a ruthlessly rational philosophy which developed his principles of mathematics into a system of logic. 'Logic', he said, 'is the youth of mathematics and mathematics is the manhood of logic.' Russell's thesis was that the combined force of logic and mathematics provided a comprehensive and objective understanding of our world and of our place within it. He held that while the existence of God and the possibility of personal immortality might be *logically* possible, there was no real basis to believe in either. He concluded that religious belief was rationally indefensible.

For philosophers of religion, as for theologians, the challenge has been the need to take account of constantly changing world-views, contact with radically different religions as well as non-religious philosophy, and event-

ually, the emergent sciences and movements such as
secularization. Like every other discipline, philosophy has
had to pass through changing cultural landscapes, while
making its own contribution to those changes. Gradually,
it became clear that the rapidly increasing range of
human knowledge would required an increasing degree
of philosophical specialization, and while philosophy was
once a more holistic and cohesive discipline, today it has
a wide-ranging curriculum. This can be outlined as: metaphysics, which is the study of the nature of reality and the
relationship of mind and body; epistemology, the nature and
range of knowledge; ethics or moral philosophy; political
philosophy, which concerns the nature of government and
social relationships; aesthetics, the study of the concept
of beauty, art and so on; logic and mathematics; the
philosophy of mind; the philosophy of language; and the
philosophy religion. A combination of all these would be
necessary in trying to put together a philosophical theory
of everything.

It is regrettable that no such cohesive philosophy exists
and that the philosophical world-view is fractured, with
many of the proponents of its various specializations in
debate with each other as to which offers the most basic
view. It was argued, for example by the American philosopher Richard Rorty, that if philosophers get their theory
of knowledge right, everything else will fall into place, or
if a philosophy of mind emerges that overcomes the old
Cartesian dualism of mind and body, it will provide a
secure foundation from which to proceed to a philosophy
of everything. The problem is compounded in that most
major disciplines have developed their own subject-
based philosophy, so we have philosophies of science, of
mathematics, religion, law and history, philosophies of
art, theatre, sociology and philosophical anthropology.
Furthermore, philosophy has found the need to be informed

by more recently emerged disciplines such as psychology and the new physics. While the traditional philosophical arguments for the existence of God have long since been abandoned, there are more telling and persuasive modern philosophers who address this belief. It is worthwhile considering examples of philosophers who are at the cutting edge of new thinking, and whose philosophies, by offering a new contribution to the God-debate, might challenge our thinking.

i) The analytic philosopher Alvin Plantinga has developed what he termed a 'reformed epistemology', that is, a revised theory of knowledge. Plantinga draws on the idea of 'reliabilism', that to hold a true belief is justified and counts as knowledge only if it is based on a reliable belief-forming process. Such a process may include psychological or philosophical validation of the kind that does not require the need for objective evidence, but which is, in Plantinga's phrase, 'properly basic'. He uses the term to argue against those who think, for example, that to believe in God is irrational. In the proposition 'I believe that God exists', it can be known that God exists, if and only if, one has arrived at that belief by means of a 'reliable process'. Plantinga holds that 'warranted, that is, knowledge-based, rational beliefs', are properly basic if they conform to certain conditions. Thus, for example, the proposition 'I believe in God', or, 'God speaks to me', may be properly basic in conditions such as those of a child who has been brought up to believe, or those of an adult who has retained religious belief despite the influence of a culture of scepticism. In such conditions it is not adequate for the atheist to say that the belief is wrong or invalid, since it is impossible for an atheist to participate in the same conditions or circumstances of belief as the believer.

In an essay entitled 'Rationality and Religious Belief',

Plantinga asks, is it rational to believe in God? It is not easy, he concedes, to say what it is for a belief to be rational. Usually what is demanded is sufficient evidence for that belief, or insufficient evidence against it. Without evidence for the belief, that belief is commonly thought to be groundless. With this Plantinga disagrees. He uses pain as an analogy. 'If I see someone displaying typical pain behaviour, I take it that he or she is in pain. Again, I don't take the displayed behaviour as *evidence* for that belief; I don't infer that belief from others I hold; I don't accept it on the basis of other beliefs. Still, my perceiving the pain behaviour plays a unique role in the formation and justification of that belief . . . it forms the ground of my justification for the belief in question.' The belief in the person's pain is taken as 'basic', because there are circumstances and conditions that provide justification for it, and which provide a ground for that belief. Transferred to the claim that God exists, the statement is valid if Plantinga's two conditions are met, that the claim is based on a 'reliable process' and is 'properly basic'. However, it is likely that the theist may have to concede that he does not know, but only believes that God exists. Plantinga's point is that belief arrived at in the way outlined above, is rational and not groundless.

ii)   The philosopher of religion D Z Phillips was primarily concerned with using philosophy as a tool to enquire into the nature of reality. Because the statement 'God exists' belongs to an order of propositions that does not rely on the usual kinds of evidence, Phillips argues that such propositions do not have what he terms a 'truth value', that is, they do not have any means by which the proposition can be related to truth. The concept of 'two-value logic', a term taken from logic and mathematics, is able to demonstrate the veracity of something simply on the grounds of whether it is true or false when that decision can be made logically. In such a case a proposition can be said to have a 'truth value'. Alternatively, intuitionist logic lacks a complete truth value system because it deals with propositions for which the criteria, truth or falsity, cannot be logically applied but for which the quality, truth, might still be used. Phillips states that propositions not having a truth value are 'a form of life'. Somewhat as did Paul Tillich (see Chapter 3), he is suggesting that the question as to whether God exists is not a proper question because it confuses both the logic and language of theism with those of other disciplines, for example, with the logic and language of science. Phillips regards the job of the philosopher is not to investigate the rationality of the claim that God exists, but to elucidate its meaning.

Phillips takes his idea of religion as 'form of life' from Wittgenstein. His argument is that if there is truth in religion, that is if it has valid meaning, that meaning can only be found in the life to which it is related and in which it is used. Wittgenstein famously argued that the meanings of the words we use are to be found in the function they have in our discourse, a principle he illustrated in his book *Culture and Value*, with reference to the tools in a tool box, 'there is a hammer, pliers, a saw, a screw-driver, a rule, a glue-pot, nails and screws . . . the function of words are as diverse as the function of these objects . . . meaning is use'.

Simply put, Phillips followed a similar argument that the truth or falsity of the God-hypothesis is not to be found by referring to the accepted meaning of words, but in the way they are used. Words, as we have seen, are tools; what they mean is determined by their function. The tradition, carried from Aristotle to Hume, had been to argue for or against the existence of God from the ground of metaphysics. Wittgenstein questioned this metaphysical premise and turned the enquiry towards the meaning and use of language, thus providing philosophers with what is termed a 'non-realistic' method. This is probably best illustrated from the sociology of religion. Phillips argues that religion today is mostly concerned with the way we live. Among the examples he gives are prayer and a belief in an afterlife; both of these are rational because the motives behind these beliefs hold together without the old metaphysical premise. Phillips suggests that to pray for the recovery of a child from illness may simply be an expression of the parents' deep anxiety and their hope that their child will get well; it does not, necessarily, mean they are asking for some remote God to suspend the laws of nature on their behalf. Phillips's contribution poses the interesting underlying question as to whether it is possible to have religion without metaphysics, and if so what kind of religion this would be. Phillips understands that religious beliefs are dependent on the *non-religious* features of human existence for their sense and importance; he suggests a kind of marriage between sacred and secular perceptions, and that the relationship between religious belief and non-religious aspects of life is one of symbiosis and not one that requires justification by evidence or argument.

iii)   The British philosopher Antony Flew was, for the greater part of his life, a convinced advocate of atheism. Late in life, just six years before his death, his atheism gave way to a form of religious belief. His stand against the God-hypothesis was traditional in that he argued that claims and belief statements about God were meaningless if the truth or falsity of them could not be tested, and that the only intellectually valid position to hold was to assume atheism until evidence for God could be produced. His change of heart was based on his revised understanding of what is termed 'intelligent design', which he found to be 'enormously stronger than it was when I first met it'.

He found the concept related to him far more relevantly than an undirected process such as natural selection. But, for Flew, the divine intelligence behind the design is not the God of the Bible, but the Aristotelian God conceived in terms of the unmoved mover related primarily to the concept of 'being', the highest determinations of which, actuality and potentiality, were discussed in Chapter 3. Interestingly, Flew was persuaded by the arguments of another English philosopher, David Conway, who pointed out that the attributes Aristotle ascribed to God, such as immutability, omniscience, omnipotence, indivisibility (oneness or unity), correspond to the attributes given to the monotheistic God of the Judeo-Christian tradition. In *Recovery of Wisdom*, Conway suggests that the 'classical conception of philosophy . . . is the view that the explanation of the world and its broad form is that it is the creation of a supreme omnipotent and omniscient intelligence, more commonly referred to as God, who created it in order to bring into existence and sustain rational beings'. The importance of this is that it adds to the God-debate the notion that we can apprehend the existence and nature of God by the exercise of unaided human reason.

The God that drew Flew out of atheism was a God that combined power with intelligence. He rejected such concepts as the afterlife, the resurrection of Jesus, and God as the source of good, charging God with being responsible for 'a lot of evil'. Flew tells his story in *There Is a God*, where he states 'the most impressive arguments for God's existence are those that are supported by recent scientific discoveries', these being the insights of the new physics about the origin of the universe. Flew would have been in close agreement with the third President of the United States, Thomas Jefferson: 'While reason, mainly in the form of arguments to design, assures us that there is a God, there is no room either for any supernatural revelation of the God or for any transactions between that God and individual human beings.' Reason and observation of the natural world made a deist of the atheist, enabling him to believe in a God without any reliance on revealed religion, or any form of religious authority, be it a priest or a book. The World Union of Deists offers a definition of modern deism as, 'the recognition of a universal creative force greater than that demonstrated by mankind, supported by personal observation of laws and designs in nature and the universe, perpetuated and validated by the innate ability of human reason coupled with the rejection of claims made by individuals and organized religions of having received special divine revelation'.

In one sense, Antony Flew's move into deism returns us to the discussion of a theory of everything since, as the South African philosopher J N Findlay put it in *Language, Truth and Value*, 'the proper object of religious reverence must in some manner be *all-comprehensive*: there mustn't be anything capable of existing, or of displaying any virtue, without owing all of these absolutely to this single source. . . . God mustn't merely cover the territory of the actual, but also, with equal comprehensiveness the territory of the possible.' This notion of God, or the divine, overcomes the dualism of essence and existence, which turns us back to the concept of pure Being that so interested Flew.

Flew tell us that his journey from atheism to theism was 'a pilgrimage of reason.' Echoing Socrates, he explained, 'I have followed the argument where it has led me. And it has led me to accept the existence of a self-existent, immutable, immaterial, omnipotent, and omniscient Being.'

2. The Scientists

Belief in the existence of God is, for many scientists, entirely compatible with their commitment to science and, in so believing, not only do they have a different perception of spirituality, they also have a different understanding of science. Arguing against the God-hypothesis, atheistic scientists mostly regard the concept of God in terms of biblical convention, whereas in the main believing scientists hold to a conception of God that is far broader and not necessarily subject to a received theological tradition or even to what is termed, 'religion.' Being able to see a relationship between the God-hypothesis and, for example, quantum theory, edges such believers towards the possibility of a more comprehensive theory of everything in which religious experience melds with, for example, the knowledge gained from evolutionary biology and astrophysics.

In Chapter 4, the case for atheism set science against religion in reference to the basic issues of creation and evolution, and the moral issues of evil and suffering. The question raised by these issues is why, for some scientists, physics and evolutionary biology exclude any possibility of the existence of God, while others find their faith confirmed by what science has disclosed. What do some scientists see and understand that remains inaccessible to their non-religious colleagues? Before responding to this question, it should be pointed out that Richard Dawkins dismisses the position held by religious scientists on the grounds of their rarity; his search for them has mostly been among those he considers to be 'eminent scientists', and his argument would have been stronger if he had considered that while the spotlight falls inevitably on the elite, their religious perception is shared by others less eminent, the users and teachers of science in laboratories and classrooms. Such believers are not necessarily found in the traditional places of worship, nor have they need for a conventional view of God. How, then, do some leading scientists reconcile a scientific and metaphysical world-view?

i)   John Polkinghorne is a theoretical physicist and theologian, disciplines he has combined as Professor of Mathematical Physics at the University of Cambridge and with ordination as an Anglican priest. As such, Professor Polkinghorne is concerned to make a relationship between science and, in his case, the Christian notion of God. This is done by a response to what he terms 'moments of radical revision', changes of perception which both scientists, theologians and philosophers have had to make. Science has been radically revised by quantum theory; theology and philosophy have been similarly recast in response to movements such as de-mythology and secularization. For many Christians, an understanding of the person and nature of Jesus Christ has had to be radically revised as the myths of virgin birth, resurrection and ascension have been peeled away to reveal the actual, historical Jesus. The sharp contrast between science and theology, Polkinghorne points out, lies in their respective responses to these kinds of 'radical revision', science 'advancing to greater understanding, the other [theology], continually wrestling with age-old problems', but both encountering mystery on the way, that is the mystery of something veiled, but set in a context science enables us to understand. In *Belief in God in an Age of Science*, he points out that, 'Quantum theory also tells us that the world is not simply objective; somehow it is something more subtle than that. In some sense it is veiled from us, but it has a structure that we can understand.' He argues that theism is needed to make total sense of the world and that 'the force of this claim depends upon the degree to which belief in God affords the best explanation of the varieties, not just of religious experience, but of all human experience'.

For Polkinghorne, one possible way to that 'best explanation' was to make a relationship between chaos theory and natural theology. Chaos theory, sometimes referred to as the 'butterfly effect', suggests that small differences in original conditions can result in widely divergent consequences in chaotic systems (such as the weather) making accurate predictions, if not impossible, then unlikely. Natural theology is a theology based on conclusions drawn by the observation of the ordinary course of nature, those conclusions being primarily of a teleological, argument-from-design type which are thought to be evidence for the existence of a 'Designer'. It has already been shown that such arguments are inadequate as a proof for God's existence (see Chapter 4): 'many natural theologians have abandoned the search for demonstrative arguments, appealing instead to ones which are probable, either in the sense of having weight but being inconclusive or in the sense of having a mathematical probability assigned to them. While there are differences of approach, the common theme is that there is evidence for theism but evidence of a probable rather than a conclusive kind, justifying belief but not full belief' (*Stanford Encyclopaedia of Philosophy*). Nevertheless, scientists such as Polkinghorne suggest that the emergence of chaos theory requires natural theology to make the radical revision referred to above. He argues that the vital relationship between them is further evidence of an intelligence running through the existence of everything, of the kind that so impressed Anthony Flew.

Today, observation of nature includes the scientist's microscopic and telescopic scrutiny of nature in all its aspects. Polkinghorne is suggesting that what is true of the mathematics of chaos is also true of nature, that we cannot know in any reliable detail the future behaviour of nature, or any quantum or chaotic system. For this reason the true nature of God, how he relates to the world and how we perceive his existence and our relationship to it, cannot be formed in any predetermined philosophical or theological system, since the 'originator' of our experience of God, drawn from an observation of nature, is so varied as to produce its own butterfly effect within our own consciousness and intuition. His point is to raise the question as to how God acts in the physical world. Polkinghorne's concept of God, although couched in Christian terms, is not a determinist God in total control of a mechanistic universe, nor is he a God who has brought order to the kind of chaos traditionally supposed to have preceded creation. Rather, his God is of the kind that might be consistent with an anthropic universe, one that was originated and has developed with the human species 'in mind', as if a place was specifically prepared for humanity, even if that 'preparation' is best described by science. Polkinghorne quotes Freeman Dyson, an American theoretical physicist and mathematician, who said that, 'the more I examine the universe and the details of its architecture, the more evidence I find that the universe, in some sense, must have known we were coming . . . which is the way it is in its anthropic fruitfulness because it is the expression of the purposive design of a Creator who has endowed it with the finely tuned potentiality for life.'

Polkinghorne offers two possible conclusions to what he admits is a metaphysically ambiguous issue: either we can read the relationship in such as away as to reduce the rich and complex structure to something that 'is merely the elaboration of a fundamental simplicity, or it can be read in a holistic way as indicating the inadequacy of a mechanical view for the task of capturing the subtle and exquisitely sensitive patterning of actual behaviour. I prefer the latter metaphysical strategy as the one more promisingly compatible with human experience.'

ii) Apart from his book *God's Undertaker – Has Science Buried God?* much of what John Lennox has had to say about the existence of God has been debated in public with the New Atheists, like Richard Dawkins and Christopher Hitchens. Lennox, a Cambridge professor of mathematics and philosophy of science, is a Christian and his defence is of the biblically-based Christian view of God. Having accused Dawkins and Hitchens of not discriminating between religions, damning them all by damning one, and of presenting a worst-case scenario of Christianity, he himself fails to take a broader religious view that might have extended the ground of his defence. Having said that, many of the arguments Lennox offers in defence of a conventional Christianity are useful arguments for the case of a more broadly based metaphysic.

Faith, he argues, is not blind but evidence-based, that evidence being deduced from science, history, morality and experience. Science provides the God-hypothesis with a form of natural theology that is supportive of theism by demonstrating a complexity that implies an intelligent designer. Lennox argues against the idea that by the process of evolution human intelligence (mind) was developed from matter (brain), insisting that mind precedes matter, and he uses the genetic code of the DNA as an illustration. He argues that the code is analogous to language, that it is a set of instructions that determines both the development and the function of an organism. His argument includes the concept of complexity. The usual scientific principle, suggested originally by Newton, is that any phenomenon should be explained in terms simpler than the phenomenon being explained. Lennox reverses this thesis, arguing that frequently the better explanation is more complex. He illustrates this from gravity, pointing out that the actual event of an apple falling is very simple, but the explanation as to why it falls down rather than up is highly complex.

Wrapped up with this argument is the distinction he makes between mechanism and agency, a distinction he claims atheists fail to apply. Lennox argues that, as we have come to understand how the mechanism of physics explains, for example, a phenomenon such as gravity, so scientists have found reason to believe that there is an agent behind that mechanism responsible for its design. It is for this reason that Lennox criticises Dawkins and others, not about their science but about their philosophy; they presume that because we fully understand a mechanism such as gravity, no agency exists. In the book mentioned above, Lennox refers to Newton's experience, 'When Sir Isaac Newton discovered the universal law of gravitation he did not say, "I have discovered a mechanism that accounts for planetary motion, therefore there is no agent, God, who designed it." Quite the opposite, precisely because he understood how it worked, he was moved to increase admiration for God who had designed it that way.' Furthermore, in failing to make the distinction between mechanism and agency, Lennox believes that atheism is guilty of a disservice to science, in that by proposing a universe conceived by a rational intelligence, Christianity has generated the scientific revolution.

Another aspect of Lennox's perception of God draws heavily on the concepts of morality and truth. He pleads that if all life is governed by the mechanical process of natural selection and the genetic code of the DNA, then the only source for human morality is our conditioning by the variable and relative values of society. The DNA, he points out, is neither good, nor bad, nor evil, and if everything we think and do is predetermined and mechanistic, we're left with a moral anarchism close to that pointed out by Dostoevsky, 'If God does not exist everything is permissible.' It follows, Lennox argues, that if we are entirely driven by our DNA, and if the forces behind that are the survival mechanisms of natural selection, what is it that directs our instincts to what is right or true, when by doing wrong, or by lying, rather than telling the truth, we may be better able to survive? If survival is not dependent on truth or the moral quality of our lives, what does this tell us of the mechanism 'that has been "created" by a mindless evolutionary process?'

Inevitably, perhaps, it is here that Lennox turns to the New Testament where he finds his thesis, that morality and truth are synonymous with God is endorsed by Jesus' 'I am the way, the truth, and the life' (John 14:6). Lennox's God, then, is not just an intelligent designer but the source of all truth and meaning, and a being with whom it is possible to have a relationship. His perception offers what is probably the most complete synthesis of science and a more conventional theology.

iii) The physicist Paul Davies has gone so far as to say that science can now offer as clear a path to God as religion. His scientific interests include astrobiology, cosmology and theoretical physics, quantum field theory and curved space-time. He was an early contributor to the theory that life on Earth originated on Mars, that it was 'cocooned' and carried in rocks thrown up by asteroid and comet impact. He is committed to the belief that science and religion are not mutually exclusive, but can engage in meaningful dialogue. For his contribution to that dialogue he was awarded the 1995 $1 million Templeton Prize for Progress in Religion. In his Templeton address he said, 'science can proceed only if the scientist adopts an essentially theological worldview'. His belief in God is based on a scientist's account of natural theology, a view he develops in his book *The Mind of God*. 'It is impossible to be a scientist,' he suggests, 'even an atheist scientist, and not be struck by the awesome beauty, harmony, and ingenuity of nature. What most impresses me is the existence of an underlying mathematical order, an order that led the astronomer Sir James Jeans, to declare, "God is a pure mathematician."' Davies is a staunch defender of the charge that science leaves us with a dehumanized world-view, a 'message of despair'; against this he argues that science and religion are, together, engaged in the same task, a search for an objective, ultimate truth, or theory of everything.

Science, Davies proposes, has changed and expanded the conceptual framework in which the debate about the existence of God takes place, while at the same time illuminating religion's own concepts about, for example, the nature and origin of the universe. For the debate to continue as a constructive dialogue, religion must be receptive to a scientific 'enlightenment'. Davies writes, 'The new physics has overturned so many common-sense notions of space, time and matter that no serious religious thinker can ignore it.' The problem is that, while physicists will happily abandon a theory in favour of an improved or better version of it, theists, to say the least, have been reluctant to relinquish the old forms of their faith for new ones. In *God and the New Physics*, Davies interestingly suggests that the 'new physicists' are reluctant to speak of 'truth', of something that is either right or wrong, since physics is about models, 'models that help us to relate one observation to another in a systematic way', and that the only reality we have is what is observed in this process. For constructive dialogue to take place between science and religion, religion must let go of the dogma on which it is founded in favour of the new conceptual models offered by science. In fairness to religion, there have been many attempts to do just this, as noted in the discussions above about de-mythology, religion and secularism, and so on. Science, Davies suggests, makes its principal contribution through reductionism, disclosing the basic and simple beauty of the structures that make up the world. For a holistic approach, the God-hypothesis is needed, since physics has nothing so say about the meaning and purpose of our lives, or about morality and aesthetics. It can tell us *how* everything exists, but it can tell us nothing about *why* anything exists.

To find the answers to these more abstract but central questions, Davies suggests that a form of mysticism might be needed. Traditionally, mysticism stands at the opposite extreme from rational, scientific thought, but since science can tell us 'how', but cannot tell us 'why', we need to call on a form of scientific mysticism. It is the claim of mysticism, both in the West and the East, that ultimate reality can be perceived, that is, experienced. It is the 'cosmic religious feeling', of which Einstein spoke. Ken Wilber explained in *Quantum Questions* that, 'in the mystical consciousness, Reality is apprehended directly and immediately, meaning without any meditation, any symbolic elaboration, any conceptualization, or any abstractions; subject and object become one in a timeless and spaceless act that is beyond any and all forms of meditation'. The language is somewhat cryptic, but what it addresses is a theory of everything that transcends the theory itself to become an experience which, if meaningful, is an experience of ultimate unity of the kind sought by the followers of Eastern religions.

In *Infinity and the Mind,* Rudolf Rucker, an American mathematician and computer scientist, explains that, 'the central teaching of mysticism is this: *Reality is One.* The practice of mysticism consists in finding ways to experience this unity directly. The One has variously been called the Good, God, the Cosmos, the Mind, the Void or . . . the Absolute. No door to the labyrinthine castle of science opens directly onto the Absolute. But if one understands the maze well enough, it is possible to jump out of the system and experience the Absolute for oneself.' Davies gives examples of scientists who have had some experience of 'jumping out of the system'; they include Roger Penrose,

Kurt Gödel, Fred Hoyle, and to some degree this is also true of the scientists discussed here. Rucker again, 'If the Mindscape is a One, then it is a member of itself, and thus can only be known through a flash of mystical vision. No rational thought is a member of itself, so no rational thought could tie the Mindscape into a One.'

Little of the above would make any sense at all to atheistic scientists who are opposed to the whole notion of metaphysics and mystical experience. There is nothing here that would enable them to engage in dialogue even with their theistic colleagues; their science they would never question, but their belief in God they find incomprehensible. But the purpose of this chapter has been to shift the usual 'right or wrong' ground of the debate, to a more open and ever-changing conceptual context. Within that context, Paul Davies cogently represents the theistic scientist point of view, 'I began by making the claim that science offers a surer path than religion in the search for God. It is my deep conviction that only by understanding the world in all its many aspects – reductionist and holist, mathematical and poetical, through forces, fields, and particles as well as through good and evil – that we will come to understand ourselves and the meaning behind the universe, our home.'

It is by no means sure that scientists will ever achieve a single, unified theory of everything or, as it is alternatively referred to somewhat eschatologically, the 'final theory'. Such a theory has been sought from Democritus, who hoped his concept of the 'atom' would lead to a unifying principle, to Stephen Hawking's 'mind of God'. In the long intervening period between them, many attempts have been made that included, for example, Archimedes, who tried to put together a putative theory based on a definitive list of axioms; Newton's *Mathematical Principles of Natural Philosophy*, which attempted a unification theory, and Laplace, the French mathematician and astronomer who suggested that a combination of the theories of gravitation and mechanics would provide a comprehensive theory. Michael Faraday endeavoured, unsuccessfully, to create a synthesis of gravity, electricity and magnetism, and Einstein searched for his unified field theory. Contemporarily, it is thought that without the inclusion of quantum mechanics no unification of the basic interactions of nature can be attempted. A new vocabulary has developed to express the new physics that includes, for example, 11-dimensional M-theory, matrix string-theory, and superstring theory. It is beyond the scope of this book to elucidate these concepts, and notwithstanding their seemingly comprehensive agenda, the current belief is that there is no likely convincing proposal that might lead to a theory of everything.

The foregoing discussions, based on the ideas of philosophers and scientists supportive of the God-hypothesis, suggest that both philosophy and theology could have a contribution to make to whatever theory of everything may, eventually, emerge. Theists argue that such a theory, based on scientific reductionism will be flawed; atheists argue that the God-hypothesis can never amount to a final, satisfying explanation.

This final chapter has outlined the principal ideas of both scientists and philosophers wanting to combine the reductionism of science with the 'expansionism' of the God concept. It is an exciting and volatile combination that provides a new platform for a perennial debate which, if it is to serve any future purpose, is best engaged creatively by means of open-minded dialogue, rather than hard-edged dogmatism. Only by such means might we understand Einstein's assertion that 'Science without religion is lame, religion without science is blind.'

Further Reading

Aristotle, *Metaphysics*, J M Dent, Everyman Edition, 1956
Augustine, Saint (trans. R S Pine-Coffin), *Confessions*, Penguin, 1970
Ayer, A J, *Language, Truth and Logic*, Pelican, 1971
Aquinas, Thomas, *Selected Philosophical Writings*, OUP, 1993
Badiou, Alain (trans. Oliver Feltham), *Being and Event: Philosophy in the Present*, Continuum, 2010
——, & Slavoj Zizek, *Philosophy in the Present*, Polity Press 2009
Baillie, John, *Our Knowledge of God*, Oxford Paperbacks, Oxford University Press, 1963
Becker, Ernest, *Escape from Evil*, Free Press, 1975
——, *The Denial of Death*, Free Press, 1997
Bonhoeffer, Dietrich, *The Cost of Discipleship*, Fontana, 1978
——, *Letters, Lectures and Notes from the Collected Works: Way Freedom*, Fount, 1972
——, *Letters and Papers from Prison*, Fontana, 1971
Buber, Martin, *I & Thou*, T & T Clarke, 1959
——, *The Eclipse of God*, Harper Torchbooks, Harper and Row, 1957
Cahn, Steven, & David Shatz, *Contemporary Philosophy of Religion*, OUP, 1982
Capra, Fritjof, *The Tao of Physics*, Flamingo, HarperCollins, 1992
Chopra, Deepak, *How to Know God*, Rider, 2001
Cohen, Hermann, *Ethics of Pure Will*, Kessinger Publishing, 2010
Collingwood, R G, *The Idea of History*, OUP, 1978
Cox, Harvey, *The Secular City*, SCM, 1965
D'Sousa, Dinesh, *What's So Great About Christianity?*, Tyndale House Publications, 2009
Davies, Paul, *God and the New Physics*, Pelican, 1988
——, *The Mind of God*, Penguin, 1992
Dawkins, Richard, *The God Delusion*, Bantam Press, 2006

Eagleton, Terry, *Reason, Faith, and Revolution: Reflections on the God Debate*, Yale University Press, 2009

Farrer, Austin, *Interpretation and Belief*, 9th edn, SPCK, 1976

Findlay, J N, *Language, Truth and Value*, Humanities Press, 1963

Flew, Anthony, *New Essays in Philosophical Theology*, SCM, 1955

——, with Roy Abraham Varghese, *There is A God*, HarperOne, 2008

Freud, Sigmund, *The Future of an Illusion*, Pacific Publishing Studio, 2010

Fuller, Richard Buckminster, *I Seem to be a Verb*, Buckminster Fuller Reader, Penguin, 1972

Gardner, Gerald, *The Meaning of Witchcraft*, Red Wheel, Samuel Weiser, 2011

Govinda, Lama, *The Foundations of Tibetan Mysticism*, Samuel Weiser, 1969

Graves, Robert, *The Greek Myths*, Penguin, 1962

Hawking, Stephen, *A Brief History of Time*, Guild Publishing, 1988

Heidegger, Martin (trans. Miles Groth), *Letter on Humanism*, PhD, on-line PDF

——, *Being and Time*, State University of New York, 1996

Hitchens, Christopher, *God Is Not Great*, Atlantic Books, 2007

Huxley, Julian, *Essays of a Humanist,* Penguin & Chatto Windus, 1966

Jeans, James, *Physics and Philosophy*, Cambridge University Press, 1948

James, William, *The Varieties Of Religious Experience*, Signet Classics, 2003

John of the Cross, St, *The Spiritual Canticles,* Harper Collins, 2004

Jung, Carl, *Psychology and Religion East and West*, Routledge & Kegan Paul, 1958

——, *Memories, Dreams and Reflections*, Collins Fount, 1963

——, *Answer to Job, The Collected Works of C J Jung*, vol. 11, Bollingen Series, 1973

Kant, Immanuel, *Prolegomena to Any Future Metaphysics*, Hackett Publishing, 1977

Kierkegaard, Soren, (ed and trans. Alexander Dru), *The Journals of Kierkegaard, 1834–1854*, Fontana, 1965

—— (ed and trans. Ronald Gregor Smith), *The Journals of Kierkegaard, 1853–55*, Collins, 1965

Küng, Hans, *On Being a Christian*, SCM, 1991

——, *The Beginning of All Things: Science and Religion*, Wm B Eerdmans, 2007

——, 'The Testimony of Faith to the Ultimate Origin', *Tikkun*, March/April 2010

Lennox, John C, *God's Undertaker: Has Science Buried God?*, Lion Books, 2009

Lewis, C S, *Mere Christianity*, Collins Fount, London, 1983

——, *Surprised by Joy*, Collins Fount, 1983

Locke, John, *An Essay Concerning Human Understanding*, Wordsworth Editions, 1998

McCabe, Joseph, *The Rationalist Encyclopedia*, Watts, 1950

Moojan Momen, *The Phenomenon of Religion: A Thematic Approach*, One World, 1999

Nicholson, Reynold, A, *The Mystics of Islam*, Routledge and Kegan Paul, 1975

O'Hear, Anthony, *After Progress*, Bloomsbury, 1999

——, *Beyond Evolution*, Clarendon Press, 1999

Otto, Rudolf, *The Idea of the Holy*, OUP, 1973

Paton, H J, *The Modern Predicament*, George Allen and Unwin, 1955

Peters, Karl E, *Dancing with the Sacred*, Trinity Press International, 2002

Plantinga, Alvin, *God and Other Minds*, Cornell University Press, 1967

Plato, *The Republic*, Macmillan, 1925

——, *The Symposium*, Penguin Classics, 1976

Polkinghorne, John, *Belief in God in an Age of Science*, Yale University Press, 1998

——, *One World*, SPCK, 1986

——, *Reason and Reality: The Relationship Between Science and Theology*, SPCK, 1991

——, *Faith of a Physicist*, Princeton University Press, 1994

Primack, Joel, *Scientists Comment on Faith*, www.thegodpod.com

Ramsey, Ian T, *Religious Language*, SCM, 1957

Robinson, John A T, *Honest to God*, SCM, 1963

Robinson, John, and David Edwards, *The Honest to God Debate*, SCM, 1963

Rogers, Carl (eds Howard Kirschenbaum & Valerie L Henderson), *The Carl Rogers Reader*, Constable, 1990

Rucker, Rudolf von Bitter, *Infinity and the Mind*, Princeton University Press, 2004

Rumi, *Selected Poems*, Penguin Classics, 1995

Sartre, Jean-Paul, *Being and Nothingness*, Philosophical Library, 1956

————, *The Imaginary: A Phenomenological Psychology of the Imagination*, Routledge Classics, 2010

Schlipp, Paul Arthur, and Maurice S Friedman (eds), *The Philosophy of Martin Buber*, Open Court, 1967

Shermer, Michael, *The Science of Good and Evil*, Holt, 2004

Schweitzer, Albert, *The Quest for the Historical Jesus*, Macmillan, 1962

Swinburne, Richard, *Is There a God?*, OUP, 2003

Tarnas, Richard, *The Passion of the Western Mind: Understanding the Ideas that Have Shaped Our World View*, Ballantine Books, 1993

Taylor, Charles, *Sources of the Self*, Harvard University Press, 1992

Taylor, C Mark, *About Religion: Economics of Faith in Virtual Culture*, University of Chicago Press, 1999

————, *After God*, University of Chicago Press, 2007

Teilhard de Chardin, Pierre, *The Phenomenon of Man*, Collins, 1983

Tillich, Paul, *The Shaking of the Foundations*, SCM, 1957

————, *The New Being*, SCM, 1956

————, *Theology of Culture*, OUP, 1980

Van Buren, Paul, *The Secular Meaning of the Gospel: Based on an Analysis of its Language*, SCM, 1963

Whitehead, A N, *Process and Reality*, Free Press, Simon and Schuster, 1979

Wilbur, Ken, *A Brief History of Everything*, Shambhala, 1996

————, *Quantum Questions*, Shambhala, 1984

Wittgenstein, Ludwig, *Culture and Value*, University of Chicago Press, 1984

Wright, Robert, *The Evolution of God*, Abacus, 2010

Yogananda, Paramahansa, *Autobiography of a Yogi*, Rider, 1994

Zukav, Gary, *The Seat of the Soul*, Simon and Schuster, 1990

Principal Authors Cited

(Where dates of birth and death are not given, it is because they are not known.)

Adams, William: Professor of Natural Philosophy, King's College, London (1836–1915)

Al-Hallaj, Mansur: Persian Sufi mystic and poet (*c.*858–922)

Anselm: Benedictine monk and philosopher (1033–1109)

Aristotle: Greek philosopher and polymath (384–322 BCE)

Aquinas, Thomas: Italian Dominican priest, philosopher and theologian (1225–74)

Augustine (of Hippo), Saint: Latin-speaking philosopher and theologian (354–430 CE)

Ayer, A J: Professor of the Philosophy of Mind and Logic, University College, London (1910–89)

Badiou, Alain: Moroccan-born French anti-postmodernist philosopher (*b.*1937)

Bakunin, Mikhail: Russian revolutionary and the 'father' of anarchist theory (1814–76)

Becker, Ernest: Cultural anthropologist and interdisciplinary scientist (1924–74)

Bentham, Jeremy: English jurist, philosopher and legal and social reformer (1748–1832)

Bergson, Henri: French philosopher of immediate experience and intuition (1859–1941)

Berkeley, George: Bishop of Cloyne; Irish philosopher of subjective Idealism (1685–1753)

Bonhoeffer, Dietrich: Lutheran pastor, theologian and martyr (1906–1945)

Buber, Martin: Jewish philosopher of dialogue and religious existentialism (1878–1965)

Bultmann, Rudolf: German theologian and Professor of New
   Testament studies at the University of Marburg (1884–1976)
Burke, Edmund: Irish statesman, political theorist and philosopher
   (1729–97)
Calvin, John: French theologian, pastor and leading figure in the
   Protestant Reformation (1509–64)
Capra, Fritjof: Austrian-born American physicist and writer
   (b.1939)
Carter, Brandon: Australian theoretical physicist (b.1942)
Cohen, Hermann: German philosopher and founder of the
   Marburg School of Neo-Kantianism (1842–1918)
Collingwood, R G: British philosopher and historian
   (1889–1943)
Comte, Auguste: French philosopher and founder of the discipline
   of sociology (1798–1857)
Conway, David: British philosopher and researcher for Civitas
   think tank, the Institute for the Study of Civil Society (b.1947)
D'Sousa, Dinesh: Christian apologist and President of King's
   College, New York (b.1961)
Davies, Paul: British physicist, Professor at Arizona State University
   (b.1946)
Dawkins, Richard: evolutionary biologist (b.1941)
Descartes, René: French philosopher and writer (1596–1650)
Eagleton, Terry: British literary theorist and critic and Professor of
   English Literature at the University of Lancaster (b.1943)
Eckhart, Meister: German theologian, philosopher and mystic
   (1260–1327)
Einstein, Albert: German-born theoretical physicist
   (1879–1955)
Epicurus: Ancient Greek philosopher (341–270 BCE)
Feuerbach, Ludwig: German philosopher and anthropologist
   (1804–1872)
Findlay, J N: South African philosopher, interested in rational
   mysticism (1903–87)
Fischer, John Martin: Professor of Philosophy at the University of
   California
Flew, Anthony: British analytic and evidentialist philosopher
   (1923–2010)
Freud, Sigmund: Austrian neurologist and founder of the discipline
   of psychoanalysis (1856–1939)
Fuller, Richard Buckminster: American systems theorist, architect,
   designer and inventor (1895–1983)

Galileo Galilei: Italian physicist, astronomer and philosopher
   (1564–1642)
Gardner, Gerald: English Wiccan and amateur anthropologist and
   archaeologist (1884–1964)
Govinda, Anagarika, Lama: teacher and writer of Tibetan
   Buddhism, Abhidharma and meditation (1898–1985)
Graves, Robert: English poet, translator and novelist
   (1895–1985)
Green, Arthur, Rabbi: Scholar of Jewish mysticism and Neo-
   Hasidism
Haldane, J B S: British-born geneticist, evolutionary biologist and
   Marxist (1892–1964)
Hawking, Stephen: Theoretical physicist and cosmologist (b.1942)
Hegel, George: German Idealist philosopher (1770–1832)
Heidegger, Martin: German Existentialist philosopher of
   phenomenology (1889–1976)
Hitchens, Christopher: Anglo-American author, columnist and
   literary critic (1949–2011)
Hoyle, Fred, Sir: English astronomer and mathematician. (1915–
   2001)
Hume, David: Scottish Empiricist philosopher, historian and
   economist (1711–76)
Huxley, Julian: English evolutionary biologist (1887–1975)
James, E O: Anthropologist and specialist in comparative religion
   (1888–1972)
James, William: psychologist and philosopher (1842–1910)
Jeans, Sir James: English physicist, philosopher and mathematician
   (1877–1946)
John of the Cross, Saint: Carmelite friar and Spanish mystic of the
   Counter-Reformation (1542–91)
Jung, Carl: Swiss psychiatrist and founder of analytical psychology
   (1875–1961)
Kant, Immanuel: German philosopher and anthropologist (1724–
   1804)
Kapleau, Philip, Roshi: Zen Buddhist teacher of the Sanbo Kyodan
   tradition (1912–2004)
Kierkegaard, Soren: Danish Existentialist philosopher, theologian
   and author (1813–55)
Krochmal, Nachman: Jewish philosopher, theologian and historian
   (1785–1840)
Küng, Hans: Swiss Catholic priest, theologian and author (b.1928)

Lacan, Jacques: French psychoanalyst and psychiatrist
(1901–81)

Leibniz, Gottfried: German philosopher and mathematician
(1646–1716)

Lennox, John: Professor of Mathematics and Philosophy of Science,
Oxford University

Lévi-Strauss, Claude: French anthropologist and ethnologist
(1908–2009)

Lewis, C S: Novelist, academic, medievalist and Christian apologist
(1898–1963)

Littlewood, James: British mathematician and analyst
(1885–1977)

Locke, John: English Enlightenment philosopher and physician
(1632–1704)

Luther, Martin: German priest, theologian and leader of the
Protestant Reformation (1483–1546)

Maimonides, Moses: medieval Jewish philosopher and physician
(1135–1204)

Marx, Karl: German philosopher, economist and revolutionary
sociologist (1818–83)

McCabe, Joseph: Roman Catholic priest who became a free-
thinker, writer and speaker (1867–1955)

Mead, Margaret: American cultural anthropologist (1901–78)

Mill, John Stuart: British philosopher of social and political theory,
economist and civil servant (1806–73)

Newton, Isaac: English physicist, astronomer, natural philosopher,
alchemist and theologian (1642–1727)

Nietzsche, Friedrich: German philosopher and classical philologist
(1844–1900)

Ockham, William: English Franciscan friar and scholastic
philosopher (1288–1348)

O'Hear, Anthony: Professor of Philosophy at the University of
Buckingham

Otto, Rudolf: Lutheran theologian and and scholar of comparative
religion (1869–1937)

Pascal, Blaise: French mathematician, philosopher and physicist
(1623–62)

Paton H J: Professor of Moral Philosophy, University of Oxford
(1887–1969)

Peters, Karl: Emeritus Professor of Religion at Rollins College,
Florida

Phillips, D Z: Leading proponent of Wittgensteinian philosophy of religion (1934–2006)

Plantinga, Alvin: Analytic philosopher of religion and Christian apologist (b.1932)

Plato: Classical Greek scholar, philosopher, mathematician and student of Socrates (428–347 BCE)

Polkinghorne, John: theoretical physicist and Anglican priest (b.1930)

Pope, Alexander: Much quoted English poet and translator of Homer (1688–1744)

Primack, Joel: Professor of physics and astrophysics at the University of California (b.1944)

Prior, A N: New Zealand-born logician and philosopher of tense and temporal logic (1914–69)

Pythagoras of Samos: Ionian philosopher, mathematician and founder of the religious movement, Pythagoreanism (c.570–c.495 BCE)

Ramsey, Ian: Bishop of Durham and Professor of Philosophy of Religion at the University of Oxford (1915–72)

Rank, Otto: Austrian psychoanalyst and therapist and colleague of Freud (1884–1939)

Rees, Martin: British cosmologist and astrophysicist (b.1942)

Reich, Wilhelm: Austrian-American psychiatrist and psychoanalyst (1897–1957)

Robinson, John: New Testament scholar and secular theologian. (1919–83)

Rogers, Carl: American humanistic psychologist (1902–87)

Rorty, Richard: American analytic philosopher and pragmatist (1931–2007)

Rousseau, Jean-Jacques: Genevan philosopher and writer (1712–88)

Rucker, Rudolf von Bitter: American mathematician, computer scientist, philosopher and science-fiction writer (b.1946)

Russell, Bertrand: British philosopher, mathematician and logician (1872–1970)

Sartre, Jean-Paul: French Existentialist philosopher, playwright, novelist, political activist (1905–80)

Schiller, Friedrich von: German poet, philosopher and playwright (1759–1805)

Schlick, Moritz: German philosopher and physicist (1882–1936)

Schweitzer, Albert: German theologian, philosopher, and medical missionary (1875–1965)

Scruton, Roger: English philosopher and writer (b.1944)

Shankara, Adi: Indian philosopher of non-duality (788–820)

Shermer, Michael: American historian of science, writer and founder of the Skeptics Society (b.1954)

Schopenhauer, Arthur: German philosopher and pessimist (1788–1860)

Smith, Joseph: American religions leader, founder of the Latter Day Saints movement (1805–44)

Spinoza, Baruch: Rationalist philosopher and formative contributor to the Enlightenment (1632–77)

Suzuki, D T: Japanese translator and writer on Buddhism, Zen and Shin (1870–1966)

Swinburne, Richard: Emeritus Professor of Philosophy, Oxford (b.1934)

Tarnas, Richard: Philosopher and cultural historian and professor of philosophy and psychology at the California Institute of Integral Studies (b.1950)

Taylor, Charles: Canadian political and social philosopher (b.1931)

Taylor, Mark: Philosopher of religion and cultural critic, and professor at Columbia University (b.1945)

Teilhard de Chardin, Pierre: French philosopher and palaeontologist (1881–1955)

Teresa of Avila, Saint: Spanish mystic and philosopher (1515–82)

Tillich, Paul: German-American theologian and philosopher (1866–1965)

Wesley, John: Church of England cleric and theologian; co-founder with his brother Charles of the Methodist movement (1703–91)

Whitehead, A N: English mathematician and philosopher (1861–1947)

Wilber, Ken: American writer on mysticism, philosophy, ecology and psychology (b.1949)

Wittgenstein, Ludwig: Austrian philosopher of logic, mathematics, mind and language (1889–1953)

Yogananda, Paramahansa: Indian yogi and guru of Kriya Yoga (1893–1952)

Young, John Zachary: English zoologist and neurophysiologist (1907–97)

Zahavi, Dan: Danish philosopher of phenomenology (b.1967)

Index